BARRON'S

Painless Junior

English

for Speakers of Other Languages

Jeffrey Strausser
José Paniza

BARRON'S

3 1336 08154 6583

SAN DIEGO PUBLIC LIBRARY
LOGAN

Dedication

This book is for Beth, Katie, and Matt. You are undeserved blessings.

Jeff

This book is dedicated with love to my wife, Betty Jo, and my daughters, Jennifer and Lauren. I would also like to thank my daughters for their help and encouragement with the book.

José

© Copyright 2008 by Barron's Educational Series, Inc.

All rights reserved.
No part of this book may be reproduced in any form, by photostat, microfilm, xerography, or any other means, or incorporated into any information retrieval system, electronic or mechanical, without the written permission of the copyright owner.

All inquiries should be addressed to:
Barron's Educational Series, Inc.
250 Wireless Boulevard
Hauppauge, NY 11788
www.barronseduc.com

ISBN-13: 978-0-7641-3984-0
ISBN-10: 0-7641-3984-3

Library of Congress Catalog No.: 2007042667

Library of Congress Cataloging-in-Publication Data

Strausser, Jeffrey.
  Painless junior English for speakers of other languages / Jeffrey Strausser, Jose Paniza.
     p. cm.
  Includes index.
  ISBN-13: 978-0-7641-3984-0 (alk. paper)
  ISBN-10: 0-7641-3984-3 (alk. paper)
  1. English language—Study and teaching (Elementary)—Foreign speakers. I. Paniza, Jose. II. Title.
  PE1128.S8854 2008
  372.65'21—dc22

                                                              2007042667

Printed in the United States of America
9 8 7 6 5 4 3 2 1

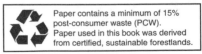

Paper contains a minimum of 15% post-consumer waste (PCW). Paper used in this book was derived from certified, sustainable forestlands.

SAN DIEGO PUBLIC LIBRARY
LOGAN

Contents

4. Putting Nouns and Pronouns into Action A Chapter about Verbs / 59

5. How Do You Describe and Compare? A Chapter about Adjectives and Adverbs / 81

6. Which Words Act Like Glue? A Chapter about Prepositions and Conjunctions / 111

7. Putting the Finishing Touches on Your Writing
A Chapter about Capitalization and Punctuation / 127

8. Do You Want to Know about Paragraphs?
A Chapter about Writing Paragraphs / 159

9. How Do You Write a Story?
A Chapter about Story Writing / 183

Introduction

MEET SHAKESPEARE, THE TEACHING CHICKEN

Hi Kids,

I'm a chicken who knows all kinds of interesting things. What kinds of things, you ask? Well, first, I know all about writing well. I will show you how to improve your English writing step by step. It's easy, and it will be fun. No boring stuff is allowed in this book!

But that's not all this chicken knows! Not only will you learn to write better, but you also will learn all kinds of cool stuff about animals—like spiders and sharks—the planets and stars, and how to be healthy and safe while you're learning to write better. Pretty cool, right?

Getting started is easy! No need to be chicken. You will start out learning about **sentences** *and the* **parts of speech***. I call these the building blocks for making a good writer. That's what you'll be—a good writer—after you have finished this book and worked all the fun exercises. This chicken knows what he is doing!*

Finally, I will show you how to write **paragraphs** *and then* **stories***. Wow! You will be amazing. You will not only be writing in English, but you will also be writing stories! That's right! Stories! And you know what? You will have had a fun time learning how to be a better writer and learning all the rest of the cool stuff that is in this book!*

Learning a new language may seem difficult at first, but this chicken knows how to make it easy. Each chapter starts out with some basic terms and definitions, and then takes you through the basics of its topic: sentences, parts of speech, paragraphs, and stories. Along the way, you may even find that what you'll learn has some similarities to your own language.

Also, to make it easier for you to learn the basics of English, I'll introduce you to some characters familiar from your own cultures, like Mr. Rodriguez and Ms. Wu. Like this chicken, they'll make the learning process fun and interesting for you. For those of you who may be new to the United States, you'll learn a lot about life in this country, including important facts about history and geography, what kinds of sports Americans like to play, and what happens in school.

Are you ready to become a better writer? I know I can hardly wait to start showing you how to do it! So, grab a notebook and a pencil and let's get started! If you have some friends who want to learn to write better, tell them you've met a teaching chicken and that you're inviting them to come along on our adventure.

Icon Key

What You'll Find...
in the chapter.

Let's Try It!
A quiz to check what
you just learned.

Think About It!
A question to test your
understanding.

Careful!
Watch out for possible
problems.

Wrapping It Up
A summary of the
chapter's main points.

Key Points!
Important ideas that you
should keep in mind.

Chapter 1

What Is There to Know about Sentences?

A Chapter about Writing Sentences

TERMS AND DEFINITIONS

Sentence: A group of words expressing a *complete thought*. That is, it tells who or what and the action that is performed.

Statement: A sentence *informing* or *telling* the reader about something.

Question: A sentence *asking* something.

Command: A sentence *telling someone to do* something.

Exclamation: A sentence *showing strong feeling.*

Subject: The part of the sentence informing the reader *who* or *what* the sentence is about.

Predicate: The part of the sentence informing the reader what the subject *is* or *is doing.*

Run-on Sentence: Two sentences incorrectly written as a single sentence.

THE SENTENCE

Sentences are important to good writing. How do you decide whether a bunch of words on paper is a sentence? What do you have to do to write a sentence? In this chapter, Shakespeare will help you learn about sentences and at the same time show you some interesting things about *animals*. Let's get started!

WHAT IS A SENTENCE?

A **sentence** is a group of words expressing a **complete thought**. That is, it tells **who** or **what** and the **action that is performed**. Let's look at some groups of words called **sentences**.

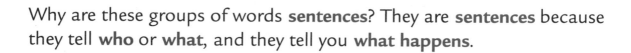

My dog's name is Rex.

I feed him and play with him every day.

Rex is a good friend.

He sleeps by my bed.

Rex likes to play in water.

Why are these groups of words **sentences**? They are **sentences** because they tell **who** or **what**, and they tell you **what happens**.

Let's look at this next group of words. These <u>are not</u> **sentences**. Can you figure out why they aren't **sentences**?

Group of Words	Why It Isn't a Sentence
My dog	It doesn't let you know **what happens** to my dog.
Plays with Yuki	It doesn't inform you **who** plays with Yuki.
Flew by me	It doesn't tell **what** flew by me.
A big bird	It doesn't show **what** the big bird does.
Is my sister	It doesn't explain **who** my sister is.

Let's Try It!
Set #1 A Trip to the Zoo

Read the group of words after each number. If the group of words makes a **sentence**, write, "This is a sentence." on the line following the words. If the group of words does not make a **sentence**, write, "This is not a sentence." on the line following the words.

Answers are on page 216.

Examples

The zoo is close to our school.   This is a sentence.
Rode on a bus to the zoo.   This is not a sentence.
The class rode on a bus to the zoo.   This is a sentence.

1. Our class went on a trip to the zoo.   _____

2. We watched the gorilla eat fruit.   _____

3. Funny monkeys.   _____

4. Swung from tree branches.   _____

5. I want to go back to the zoo.   _____

Think About It!
Set #2 More Fun at the Zoo

The following groups of words <u>are not</u> **sentences**. *Do you know why?* Let's make them into **sentences** by choosing from the group of words listed at the beginning of the exercise. Write the words you select on the line before or after each group of words below to make the group of words a **sentence**.

Remember: The first word of a **sentence** must begin with a **capital letter**.

Answers are on page 216.

a. My friends and I

b. The lions and tigers

c. has a lot of big animals

d. follow their mother

e. are swinging from branch to branch

1. The zoo _____.

2. The tiger cubs _____.

3. _____eat only meat.

4. Some of the monkeys _____.

5. _____waved to the monkeys.

Careful!

Remember every sentence must begin with a capital letter.

Key Points!

> A *sentence* is a group of words expressing a *complete thought*. A *sentence* tells <u>who</u> or <u>what</u> and the <u>action that is performed</u>.
>
> I play with my dog.
>
> My dog chases a ball.
>
> My dog likes to play with me.

KINDS OF SENTENCES

Now that you can spot sentences, let's learn about the four different kinds of sentences. Listed below are the **four kinds of sentences**.

- Statements
- Questions
- Commands
- Exclamations

STATEMENTS

A **statement** is a sentence informing the reader about something. A **statement** ends with a *period* (.). The sentences below are examples of **statements**.

German shepherds have pointed ears.

Bassett hounds have long, floppy ears.

Greyhounds are fast runners.

Chihuahuas are small dogs.

QUESTIONS

A **question** is a sentence **asking** something. A **question** ends with a *question mark* (?). A **question** usually begins with one of the following words: *Who, What, When, Where, Why,* or *How*. The sentences below are examples of **questions**.

Where is the zoo?

What is your favorite animal?

Who is going to the zoo?

When does the zoo close?

Why are the monkeys screeching?

How do the animals get food?

Let's Try It!
Set #3 Polar Bears

Change each **statement** into a **question**. Write your **question** on the line following the statement. **Questions** usually begin with one of these words: *Who, What, When, Where, Why,* or *How.*

Some possible answers are on page 216.

Examples

Polar bears live near the North Pole.	*Where* do polar bears live?
Polar bears eat seals and fish.	*What* do polar bears eat?
Polar bears are about 4 feet tall.	*How* tall are polar bears?
Polar bears are excellent swimmers.	*Who* are excellent swimmers?

1. Polar bears live where it is very cold. _____

2. A polar bear's fur is white. _____

3. Male polar bears are between 7 and 10 feet long. _____

4. A polar bear usually gives birth to two cubs. _____

5. Humans should try not to bother polar bears. _____

COMMANDS

A **command** is a sentence **telling someone to do something. A command** ends with a *period* (.). The sentences below are examples of **commands**.

Ugo, please meet me by the bears.

Don't make a lot of noise around the animals.

Rosa, look at the hawk sitting in the tree.

Don't feed the animals.

Exclamations

An **exclamation** is a sentence showing **strong feeling**, such as excitement, surprise, or fear. An **exclamation** ends with an *exclamation point* (!). The sentences below are examples of **exclamations**.

Watch out, Khanh!

I really had a good time at the zoo!

The tiger is running toward us!

This is fun!

Think About It!
Set #4 Taking Care of a Pet

Complete each sentence about taking care of a pet as either an **exclamation** or a **command**. Use the words provided below to complete each sentence by writing the correct words on the line at the beginning or end of the sentence.

Hint: The end mark will show you whether the sentence is an **exclamation** or a **command**.

Remember: The first word of a sentence must begin with a **capital letter**.

Answers are on page 216.

Examples

My dog has grown so big!   (Exclamation)
Don't feed your pet table scraps.   (Command)
Our bird is so loud!   (Exclamation)
Please feed the cat.   (Command)

a. please clean   b. dog   c. chasing a mouse
d. please pour   e. is huge

1. Bonita, walk your _____.

2. My cat is _____!

3. _____ water in your dog's bowl.

4. My dog _____!

5. _____ your hamster's cage.

Key Points!

Remember that every sentence must have an *end mark*. The *end mark* can be a period, a question mark, or an exclamation point.

A sentence's *end mark* shows you the type of sentence you are reading.

Commands and *statements* end with periods (.).
Questions end with question marks (?).
Exclamations end with exclamation points (!).

Always use the correct *end mark* for the type of sentence you have written.

Think About It!
Set #5 Sharks

On the line following each sentence, write whether the sentence is a **statement**, **question**, **command**, or **exclamation**.

Answers are on page 216.

Examples

Sharks live an average of 25 years.	statement
Have you ever seen a shark?	question
Its teeth are scary!	exclamation
Listen to the shark story.	command

1. Do you want to learn about sharks? _____

2. Great White Sharks can grow up to 14 feet long. _____

3. That is a big fish! _____

4. Whale Sharks have 300 rows of teeth. _____

5. Don't go in water where sharks are swimming. _____

SUBJECTS AND PREDICATES

Every sentence has two parts: a **subject** and a **predicate**.

SUBJECTS

The **subject** is the part of a sentence informing the reader **who** or **what** the sentence is about. In the sentences below, the **subject** of each sentence is underlined.

<u>The tiger</u> has large, sharp teeth.

<u>Gorillas and chimpanzees</u> have large hands.

<u>A toad</u> is an *amphibian*.

Let's Try It!
Set #6 Butterflies

For each of the sentences below, <u>underline</u> the **subject**.

Answers are on page 216.

Examples

<u>We</u> are learning about butterflies in science class.
<u>My friends and I</u> think butterflies are beautiful.
<u>Butterflies</u> like warm weather.

1. Butterflies have three body parts: a *head*, a *thorax*, and an *abdomen*.

2. The *thorax* is the butterfly's chest.

3. Maria and I counted six legs on a butterfly.

4. All butterflies have two sets of wings.

5. The wings and legs are connected to the thorax.

PREDICATES

The **predicate** is the part of the sentence informing the reader what the subject **is** or **what it does**. In the sentences below, the **predicate** of each sentence is <u>double-underlined</u>.

The rabbit <u>hops over the rocks</u>.

The snake <u>slithers through the grass</u>.

The shark <u>swims in the ocean</u>.

My dog <u>is very big</u>.

Jose's dog <u>is funny-looking</u>.

Let's Try It!
Set #7 Spiders

For each of the sentences below, <u>double-underline</u> the **predicate**.

Answers are on page 217.

Examples

Our teacher, Mr. Vu, <u>told us about spiders</u>.

Mr. Vu <u>teaches the third grade</u>.

He <u>is very nice</u>.

1. We learned that there are thousands of different kinds of spiders in the world.

2. Spiders have eight legs.

3. Insects have six legs.

4. Spiders are not insects but rather are *arachnids*.

5. Spiders trap insects in their webs.

Key Points!

Every *sentence* must express a complete *thought*.

Every *sentence* must have a <u>subject</u> and a <u>predicate</u>.

The <u>subject</u> informs the reader *who* or *what* the sentence is about.

The <u>predicate</u> lets the reader know what the subject *is* or *does*.

Think About It!
Set #8 More about Spiders

Complete the following sentences and learn about spiders. Draw a line to match each <u>**subject**</u> to its <u>**predicate**</u>. After you have done this, write the complete sentences on the lines below. The first sentence has been done for you.

Answers are on page 217.

Subject	**Predicate**
1. *Spiders*	cover each of a spider's legs.
2. *Webs*	is at the end of each of a spider's legs.
3. *Arachnid*	have eight legs.
4. *A tiny foot*	is another name for spider.
5. *Thick brushes of hair*	help spiders trap insects.

1. *Spiders* have eight legs. _____

2. _____

3. _____

4. _____

5. _____

WATCH OUT FOR RUN-ONS!

A **run-on sentence** is two sentences incorrectly written as one sentence. The following are examples of **run-on sentences**.

Jose owns a dog Ugo owns a cat.

The dog's name is Max the cat's name is Felix.

Max likes to chase a ball Felix likes to sleep.

Run-on sentences make your writing hard to understand because you have too many ideas in one sentence not separated by punctuation. Too many ideas written together will confuse your reader. You must correct **run-on sentences** so your reader doesn't get confused.

CORRECTING RUN-ON SENTENCES

There are two ways to correct a run-on sentence. Use the one that works best for you.

1. Split the run-on sentence into two sentences.

Separate the **run-on sentence** into two or more sentences and then use end marks (periods, question marks, and exclamation points) and capital letters to write two complete sentences. You can separate each of the **run-on sentences** written earlier into two separate sentences.

Jose owns a dog.
Ugo owns a cat.
The dog's name is Max.
The cat's name is Felix.
Max likes to chase a ball.
Felix likes to sleep.

or

2. <u>Correctly punctuate the run-on sentence.</u>

<u>After the first sentence</u>, add a *comma* (,) and the word *and* to make one complete sentence. By doing this, you can write the **run-on sentences** written earlier like this:

Jose owns a dog, *and* Ugo owns a cat.
The dog's name is Max, *and* the cat's name is Felix.
Max likes to chase a ball, *and* Felix likes to sleep.

Careful!

You must use a comma (,) followed by the word *and* when correctly punctuating a run-on sentence.

Let's Try It!
Set #9 Eagles

Use what you have just learned to correct each of the following **run-on sentences**. Write the corrected sentence or sentences on the line below each **run-on sentence**.

Answers are on page 217.

Examples

The bald eagle is a beautiful bird the bald eagle is our national bird.
The bald eagle is a beautiful bird. The bald eagle is our national bird.

There are nearly 70,000 bald eagles over half of them live in Alaska.
There are nearly 70,000 bald eagles, *and* over half of them live in Alaska.

A *salmon* is a kind of fish there are a lot of salmon in Alaska.
A *salmon* is a kind of fish. There are a lot of salmon in Alaska.

Alaska is a state in the United States many different kinds of animals live there.
Alaska is a state in the United States, *and* many different kinds of animals live there.

1. Lots of salmon live in the rivers of Alaska bald eagles like to eat salmon.

   _____

2. The bald eagle is not really bald it has white feathers on the top of its head.

   _____

3. At one time in the English language, the word "bald" meant white that is why they were named *bald eagles*.

   _____

4. A female bald eagle grows to a height of 36 inches she is taller than the male eagle.

_____

5. Eagles have wingspans of nearly 90 inches that's long!

_____

Wrapping It Up!

A *sentence* is a group of words expressing a complete thought. That is, it tells *who* or *what* and the *action* that is performed.

There are four kinds of sentences: *statements*, *questions*, *commands*, and *exclamations*.

Every sentence must have a *subject* and a *predicate* and an *end mark*.

Run-on sentences are not correct English, and they are confusing. They must be corrected by either (1) separating the *run-on sentence* into two sentences or (2) correctly punctuating the *run-on sentence* by adding a comma (,) followed by the word *and* after the first sentence.

Chapter 2

How Do You Name Persons, Places, and Things?

A Chapter about Nouns

TERMS AND DEFINITIONS

Noun: A word naming a *person*, *place*, or *thing*. A **noun** can also name a *feeling* or a *quality*.

Singular Noun: A noun naming <u>just one</u> *person*, *place*, or *thing*.

Plural Noun: A noun naming <u>more than one</u> *person*, *place*, or *thing*.

Proper Noun: A noun naming a particular person, place, or thing. A **proper noun** begins with a capital letter.

Common Noun: A noun not naming a particular *person*, *place*, or *thing*. A **common noun** does not begin with a capital letter.

Possessive Noun: The form a noun takes to show it *owns* something.

Singular Possessive Noun: The form a <u>singular noun</u> takes to show it *owns* something.

Plural Possessive Noun: The form a <u>plural noun</u> takes to show it *owns* something.

NOUNS

Nouns are important words because they are the words naming people, places, and things. In this chapter, Shakespeare will help you learn about these important words, and at the same time talk to you about something all of us have—*a family*.

WHAT IS A NOUN?

A **noun** is a word naming a *person*, *place*, or *thing*. **Nouns** are what we use to talk and write about each other and the places and things around us.

My **name** is **Juan**.

I live in **El Paso**, **Texas**.

I am a **student** at **Rodriguez Elementary School**.

SINGULAR NOUNS

A **noun** naming <u>just one</u> *person*, *place,* or *thing* is called a **singular noun**. All of the words in the box below are **singular nouns**.

Person	Place	Thing
boy	home	ball
father	school	car
son	zoo	pencil
mother	playground	pen
aunt	California	book
Maria	United States	bicycle
Ms. Wu	New York City	television
Uncle Jorge	Horner Elementary School	backpack

The *nouns* in the sentences below are in **bold**.

Maria lives in **New York City**.

The **boy** and his **aunt** are at the **zoo**.

The **pen** and the **book** are at **school**.

The **mother** and **father** sat in the **car**.

Uncle Jorge is from **El Salvador**.

Ms. Wu is a **teacher** at **Horner Elementary School**.

Let's Try It!
Set #1 Rosa and Her Family

<u>Underline</u> the **singular noun** or **singular nouns** in each of the sentences below.

Answers are on page 217.

Examples

My <u>name</u> is <u>Rosa</u>.
My <u>father</u> was born in <u>El Salvador</u>.
He works in an <u>office</u>.
My <u>mother</u> works in a <u>restaurant</u>.

1. My sister was born in El Salvador.

2. Her name is Sylvia.

3. My family lives in Los Angeles, California.

4. We live on Third Street in Los Angeles.

5. My sister and I go to Rodriguez Elementary School.

Think About It!
Set #2 My Family

Now it's your turn to use **nouns** to write about <u>your family</u>. Write the **noun** on the line for each sentence below telling something about the people in your family, where you live, and where you go to school. Use the sentences in Set #1 as a guide.

Some possible sample answers are on page 217.

1. My mother was born in _____.

2. My mother's name is _____.

3. My family lives in _____.

4. We live on _____.

5. I go to _____School.

Besides naming a person, place, or thing, a **noun** can also name a *feeling* or a *quality*. The words in the following table are **nouns** naming a *feeling* or a *quality*.

Feeling	Quality
happiness	courage
sadness	freedom
anger	bravery
fun	humility
love	modesty

My parents have **hope** for us.

We should not live in **fear**.

Anger can cause problems.

We have a lot of **fun** in Ms. Wu's class.

Careful!

Remember a <u>noun</u> can name a *person*, *place*, *thing*, *feeling*, or *quality*.

Let's Try It!

Set #3 Living in the United States

<u>Underline</u> the **noun** or **nouns** in each of the sentences below. Be careful to look for **nouns** naming *feelings* and *qualities*.

Answers are on page 218.

Examples

There is much <u>happiness</u> in my <u>family</u>.

The <u>class</u> has a lot of <u>fun</u>.

My <u>parents</u> love the <u>freedom</u> of the <u>United States.</u>

1. There is much love in my family.

2. After my grandmother died, there was much sadness.

3. Honesty is important in a family.

4. My brother had a lot of fun at the pool.

5. My mother is filled with joy and hope.

Key Points!

A *noun* can name the following:

person	(man)
place	(school)
thing	(desk)
quality	(courage)
feeling	(happiness)

PLURAL NOUNS

As we just learned, a **singular noun** is a word naming just one person, place, or thing. A **plural noun** is a word naming <u>more than one</u> person, place, or thing.

For many nouns, you can change singular nouns into **plural nouns** simply by adding -s to the end of the singular noun.

Singular	Plural
book	books
dog	dogs
brother	brothers
uncle	uncles
pencil	pencils
aunt	aunts
car	cars
sister	sisters
cousin	cousins
teacher	teachers
cat	cats

The **pencil** is on the desk.   (singular noun)
The **pencils** are all over the floor.   (plural noun)

My **sister** is in the fifth grade.   (singular noun)
My **sisters** are older than me.   (plural noun)

My mother's **brother** is my uncle.   (singular noun)
My mother's **brothers** are my uncles.   (plural noun)

Our **car** is in the garage.   (singular noun)
There are a lot of **cars** on the street.   (plural noun)

Let's Try It!
Set #4 More about Families

Write the **plural noun** of the <u>underlined</u> singular noun in the first sentence on the line at the end of the second sentence.

Answers are on page 218.

Examples

Erica has one <u>**aunt**</u>. I have four **aunts.**
Phoebe has one **cousin**. Maria has no <u>cousins</u>.

1. Sylvia has one <u>brother</u>. Ugo has two _____.

2. Jose has one <u>cousin</u>. I have three _____.

3. John has one <u>brother</u>. Maria has three _____.

4. Paulo has one <u>aunt</u>. Mateo has two _____.

5. I have one <u>uncle</u>. You have no _____.

Think About It!
Set #5 My Family

Now it is your turn again to write about *your family*! Write the number of relatives you have in each sentence on the line provided and then select the correct **singular noun** or **plural noun** in parentheses ( ) and write it on the line.

Some possible answers are on page 218.

Examples

I have _____ (brother, brothers)
I have three brothers.

I have _____ (aunt, aunts)
I have one aunt.

I have _____ (cousin, cousins)
I have no cousins.

1. I have _____ (brother, brothers)

2. I have _____ (sister, sisters)

3. I have _____ (aunt, aunts)

4. I have _____ (uncle, uncles)

5. I have _____ (cousin, cousins)

MORE PLURAL NOUNS

For a **singular noun** ending in -ss, -x, -ch, or -sh, **add** -es at the end of the **singular noun** to form the **plural noun**.

Singular Noun	Plural Noun
glass	glasses
fox	foxes
bench	benches
box	boxes
dish	dishes
wish	wishes

The **glass** is on the table.   (singular noun)
The **glasses** are on the table. (plural noun)

The girls sit on the **bench**.   (singular noun)
The girls sit on the **benches**. (plural noun)

Maria broke a **dish**.   (singular noun)
Maria broke two **dishes**. (plural noun)

Let's Try It!

Set #6 Writing Singular and Plural Nouns

Fill in the table below by selecting the correct **singular noun** or **plural noun**.

Answers are on page 218.

Singular Noun	Plural Noun
box	
	sandwiches
class	
wrench	
	foxes
bush	
	churches
mess	
	benches
dish	

SPECIAL PLURAL NOUNS

Nouns ending in -y form their **plurals** in a special way. For a singular noun ending in -y, add -ies to the singular noun to form the **plural noun**.

Singular Noun	Plural Noun
story	stories
cherry	cherries
berry	berries
party	parties
lady	ladies

Ms. Wu read us a **story**.   (singular noun)
Ms. Wu read us two **stories**.   (plural noun)

That **lady** is my aunt.   (singular noun)
Those **ladies** are my aunts.   (plural noun)

Angela had fun at the **party**.   (singular noun)
Angela had fun at the **parties**.   (plural noun)

Some singular nouns change their entire spellings to form **plural nouns**.

Singular Noun	Plural Noun
foot	feet
man	men
child	children
woman	women

That **man** is my uncle.   (singular noun)
Those **men** are my uncles.   (plural noun)

There is one **child** in my family.   (singular noun)
There are three **children** in my family.   (plural noun)

Careful!

Some singular nouns form their plural nouns differently from others. Try to learn a variety of singular nouns, and also try to learn how they form their plural nouns.

Let's Try It!

Set #7 Writing Special Plural Nouns

Complete each sentence with the **plural form of the noun** in the parentheses ( ). Write your new sentence on the line provided below.

Answers are on page 218.

Examples

Those two _____ over there are sisters. (woman)
Those two <u>women</u> over there are sisters.

We like to pick _____. (berry)
We like to pick <u>berries</u>.

1. Our teacher read us three _____. (story)

   _____

2. My shoes are on my _____ . (foot)

   _____

3. My sister went to two birthday _____. (party)

_____

4. This pie has a lot of _____. (cherry)

_____

5. The _____(man) were kicking the ball.

_____

Key Points!

Singular nouns form their *plurals* in different ways.

Most singular nouns form their *plurals* by adding -s at the end.

      mother   mothers   brother   brothers

Singular nouns ending in -ss, -x, -ch, or -sh form their *plurals* by adding -es at the end.

      box   box*es*   bench   bench*es*

Singular nouns ending in -y form their *plurals* by adding -ies at the end.

      berry   berr*ies*   cherry   cherr*ies*

Some singular nouns completely change their spellings to become *plurals*.

      child   children   man   men

Think About It!

Set #8 Using Plural Nouns to Review Sentences

In Chapter 1, you learned about the four different kinds of sentences: **exclamatory**, **question**, **command**, and **declarative**. This exercise will help you review sentence types and learn how to make **plural nouns** from singular nouns.

In the sentences below, write the **plural noun** of the singular noun in parentheses ( ) on the blank line before the singular noun. After you have finished, write the **type of sentence** on the line provided at the end of the sentence. Look back to Chapter 1 to review if you need to.

Answers are on page 218.

Examples

Watch out, _____! (boy)   _____

Watch out, <u>boys</u>!   <u>exclamatory</u>

Are the _____ (church) on this street?   _____

Are the <u>churches</u> on this street?   <u>question</u>

Please wipe your _____. (foot)   _____

Please wipe your <u>feet</u>.   <u>command</u>

The _____ (child) are in school.   _____

The <u>children</u> are in school.   <u>declarative</u>

1. Where are your _____ ? (brother) _____

2. Watch out, _____ ! (lady) _____

3. Please stop eating the _____. (berry) _____

4. The _____ (church) are on this street. _____

5. Where are the _____ (box) of crayons? _____

PROPER AND COMMON NOUNS

PROPER NOUNS

A noun naming a <u>particular</u> person, place, or thing is called a **proper noun**. A **proper noun** must begin with a *capital letter*. The nouns in the box below are examples of **proper nouns**.

Person	Place	Thing
Sylvia	United States	Monday
Ms. Ewebonike	Texas	August
Joshua	Johnson Elementary School	New Year's Eve
Abraham Lincoln	Disneyworld	Fourth of July

Careful!

Remember to *capitalize* <u>proper nouns</u>.

COMMON NOUNS

A noun <u>not naming</u> a particular person, place, or thing is called a **common noun**. A **common noun** <u>does not</u> begin with a *capital letter*. The nouns written in **bold** below are **common nouns**.

Sylvia lives in an **apartment**.

Joshua is my **brother**.

My **father** likes to work on **cars**.

Let's Try It!
Set #9 Angelina and Her Family

In the sentences below, <u>underline</u> the **common nouns** and <u>double-underline</u> the **proper nouns**.

Answers are on page 218.

Examples

My <u>name</u> is <u>Angelina</u>.

I am in the <u>third grade</u> at <u>Rodriguez Elementary School</u>.

1. My mother's name is Erika.

2. Our family lives in Texas.

3. My father is from Kenya.

4. My mother was born in the United States.

5. Our favorite month is October because we like Halloween.

Key Points!

A *proper noun* <u>does</u> name a particular person, place, or thing.

Ms. Vu Houston Condit Elementary School

A *common noun* <u>does not</u> name a particular person, place, or thing.

teacher city school

POSSESSIVE NOUNS

A **possessive noun** is a noun showing *who* or *what* <u>owns</u> something.

SINGULAR POSSESSIVE NOUNS

You can make a singular noun into a **singular possessive noun** by adding an apostrophe (') before adding *-s*.

Singular Noun	Plural Noun
boy	boy's
school	school's
father	father's
mother	mother's

The **boy's** bicycle is red.

The **girl's** dress is pretty.

My **father's** name is Jorge.

My **mother's** purse is black.

 **Let's Try It!**
Set #10 Our Relatives

<u>Underline</u> the **singular possessive noun** in each sentence.

Answers are on page 219.

Examples

My <u>mother's</u> mother is my grandmother.
My <u>cousin's</u> father is my uncle.
My <u>father's</u> mother is my grandmother.

1. My mother's sister is my aunt.

2. My father's brother is my uncle.

3. My father's sister is also my aunt.

4. My uncle's son and daughter are my cousins.

5. My aunt's son and daughter are my cousins.

PLURAL POSSESSIVE NOUNS

You can make a plural noun into a **plural possessive noun** by adding an apostrophe (') <u>after</u> the -s.

Singular Noun	Plural Noun
boys	boys'
girls	girls'
mothers	mothers'
fathers	fathers'

The **boys'** soccer uniforms are red and white.

The **girls'** dresses are blue.

The **mothers'** voices are pretty.

The **fathers'** jobs are in the same restaurant.

Careful!

Nouns form their *singular possessives* by first adding an apostrophe (') and then adding -*s*. Nouns form their *plural possessives* by first adding -*s*, and then adding an apostrophe (').

Let's Try It!

Set #11 Plural Possessive Nouns

Use the **possessive form** of the **plural noun** in parentheses ( ) at the end of each sentence. Write your new sentence on the line provided.

Answers are on page 219.

Examples

The_____ toys were on the floor. (girls)

The **girls'** toys were on the floor.

My _____ friends make a lot of noise. (sisters)

My **sisters'** friends make a lot of noise.

1. My _____ brother is my father. (uncles)

    _____

2. My _____ names are Obi and Ugo. (brothers)

    _____

3. My _____ names are Kayla and Karla. (sisters)

    _____

4. The _____ uniforms are red and white. (boys)

    _____

5. The _____ desks are messy. (teachers)

    _____

Key Points!

A *possessive noun* is a noun showing who or what *owns* something.

You can change a singular noun into a *singular possessive* noun by adding an apostrophe (') <u>before</u> adding -*s*.

boy	boy's
sister	sister's

This coat is the <u>boy's</u> coat.
My <u>sister's</u> name is Elsa.

You can change a plural noun into a *plural possessive* noun by adding an apostrophe (') <u>after</u> the -*s*.

boys	boys'
sisters	sisters'

These coats are the <u>boys'</u> coats.
The <u>sisters'</u> backpacks are on the table.

Think About It!
Set #12 My Relatives

<u>Underline</u> the **possessive noun** in each sentence. Write an **S** on the line if the **possessive noun** is *singular*. Write a **P** if the **possessive noun** is *plural*.

Answers are on page 219.

39

Examples

My <u>mother's</u> sister is my aunt.   <u>S</u>
My <u>cousins'</u> father is my uncle.   <u>P</u>
My <u>father's</u> sister is my aunt.   <u>S</u>
My <u>brothers'</u> brother is me.   <u>P</u>

1. My mother's mother is my grandmother. _____

2. My grandmother's son is my father. _____

3. My father's father is my grandfather. _____

4. My father's brother is my uncle. _____

5. My uncles' daughters are my cousins. _____

Wrapping It Up!

A *noun* is a word naming a <u>person</u>, <u>place</u>, or <u>thing</u>.

    father   school   pencil

Besides naming a person, place, or thing, a *noun* can also name a <u>feeling</u> or a <u>quality</u>.

    happiness   courage   anger

A *singular noun* is a word naming <u>just one</u> person, place, or thing.

    father   school   pencil

A *plural noun* is a word naming <u>more than one</u> person, place, or thing.

    fathers   schools   pencils

Nouns form their <u>plurals</u> in different ways.

boy	boys
cherry	cherries
man	men

A noun naming a particular person, place, or thing is called *a proper noun*.

Juan   San Francisco   Rodriguez Elementary School

A noun not naming a particular person, place, or thing is called a *common noun*.

boy   city   school

A *possessive noun* is a noun showing who or what *owns* something.

You can change a singular noun into a *singular possessive noun* by adding an apostrophe (') and then adding -*s*.

Maria's dog
school's bell

You can change a plural noun into a *plural possessive noun* by adding an apostrophe (') after the -*s*.

girls' dogs
uncles' cars

Chapter 3

What Can You Use Instead of a Noun?

A Chapter about Pronouns

TERMS AND DEFINITIONS

Pronoun: A word that can take the place of a *noun*.

Subject Pronoun: A *pronoun* acting as the *subject* of a sentence. It describes who or what the sentence is about.

Object Pronoun: A *pronoun* that follows an action verb and receives the action of the sentence.

Possessive Pronoun: A *pronoun* showing it *owns* something.

PRONOUNS

WHAT IS A PRONOUN?

Remember from Chapter 2 that a *noun* is a word naming a person, place, thing, idea, or quality? In this chapter, we are going to learn about **pronouns**. A **pronoun** is a word that can take the place of a noun. In this chapter, Shakespeare will help you to learn about **pronouns** and at the same time tell you some important things about *staying safe where you live and when you go outdoors.*

Pronouns can take the place of *proper nouns* and *common nouns*, which represent one or more persons, places, or things. Below are some examples of pronouns:

I	me
she	he
her	him
it	we
us	they
you	them

Pronouns are important to good writing because they make it more interesting. Let's see how they do this. Here is an example of writing without using any **pronouns**.

WITHOUT PRONOUNS

Jose wants Elsa to lend Elsa's book to Jose.

Maria helps Elsa with Elsa's spelling words.

Ugo wants Obi and Juan to give Ugo a piece of paper.

Did you notice how difficult these sentences are to read? They are difficult to read because they repeat the same nouns. Imagine reading an entire story written like this!

Let's see how **pronouns** can improve the sentences you have just read.

WITH PRONOUNS

Jose wants Elsa to lend **her** book to **him.**

Maria helps Elsa with **her** spelling words.

Ugo wants **us** to give **him** a piece of paper.

Let's Try It!

Set #1 Water Safety

<u>Underline</u> the **pronoun** or **pronouns** in the following sentences.

Answers are on page 219.

Examples

"<u>I</u> like to go swimming," said Carla.

"<u>**You**</u> should never swim by yourself," Juan said to Carla.

"<u>I</u> never swim by myself," Carla said to **him**.

"<u>**We**</u> always go swimming with an adult," said Carla and Bonita.

"When my friends go swimming, <u>**they**</u> always go with an adult," said Carla.

1. My father is teaching me to swim.

2. He wants me to be safe when I am in the water.

3. You should always wear a life jacket when you ride in a boat.

4. It will help you float if you fall into the water.

5. We should learn how to be safe in the water.

Think About It!

Set #2 Water Safety and Your Family

Unscramble the words to make a sentence. Write your sentence on the line provided. <u>Underline</u> the **pronoun** in each of the sentences you wrote.

Answers are on page 219.

Examples

careful be You should water around

<u>**You**</u> should be careful around water.

learning am I swim to
<u>I</u> am learning to swim.

father is My helping me
<u>My</u> father is helping me.

1. ride I my in uncle's boat

_____

2. He life jacket wears a

_____

3. sister My and I wear too one

_____

4. save can It your life

_____

5. should learn We about safety water

_____

SUBJECT PRONOUNS

The **subject** of a sentence describes *who* or *what* the sentence is about. Sometimes a **pronoun** is the **subject** of the sentence. This **pronoun** is called a **subject pronoun**. **Subject pronouns** can be singular or plural. The following table lists some **subject pronouns**.

Singular	Plural
I	we
you	you
he	they
she	
it	

I enjoy going to the lake.

"**You** should be careful around the water," said my father.

He wears a life jacket.

She also wears a life jacket.

It can save your life if **you** fall into the water.

We always practice water safety.

You can have fun and still be safe.

They are enjoying learning about water safety.

Let's Try It!
Set #3 More Water Safety

Use a **subject pronoun** from the list below to replace the underlined **noun** or **nouns** in the following sentences. Write your new sentence on the line provided.

Answers are on page 219.

I   you   he   she   we   they   it

Examples

<u>Uncle Jorge</u> is taking us out in his boat.
He is taking us out in his boat.

<u>Luisa and Isis</u> are excited.
They are excited.

Isis is wearing sunglasses.
She is wearing sunglasses.

Armando is wearing a life jacket.
He is wearing a life jacket.

1. "<u>Luisa</u> must wear a life jacket," <u>Uncle Jorge</u> said.

   _____

2. <u>Luisa</u> put on her life jacket.

   _____

3. "<u>The life jacket</u> will help me float if I fall out of the boat," <u>Luisa</u> said.

   _____

4. <u>My friends</u> should always be with an adult when they are near the water.

   _____

5. <u>Luisa and I</u> enjoy riding in Uncle Jorge's boat.

   _____

Careful!

Make sure your listener or reader will know who or what you are talking about when you replace a *noun* with a *pronoun*. If it is not clear who or what the pronoun is replacing, use the *noun*.

OBJECT PRONOUNS

Some pronouns follow *action verbs* and words like *be, for, at, to,* and *with* in a sentence. We say they <u>receive the action</u> of the sentence, and we call them **object pronouns**. **Object pronouns** can be **singular** or **plural**. The following table lists some **object pronouns**.

Singular	Plural
me	us
you	you
him	them
her	
it	

My parents don't *allow* <u>**me**</u> to play with fireworks.

"Fireworks can *burn* <u>**you**</u>," said my mother.

My mother also *told* <u>**us**</u> not to play with matches.

My mother would not *give* <u>**him**</u> matches.

Because matches can be dangerous, children should not *use* **them**.

Careful!

The *subject pronoun* <u>performs the action</u> of the sentence.
The *object pronoun* <u>receives the action</u> of the sentence.

Let's Try It!

Set #4 Fire Safety in Our Homes

<u>Underline</u> the **object pronoun** in each of the sentences below.

Answers are on page 220.

Examples

A firefighter came to our school to teach **<u>us</u>** about fire safety.

My parents want **<u>us</u>** to know what to do in case of a fire.

My mother showed **<u>me</u>** where the smoke alarm is located.

Now I know where **<u>it</u>** is located.

1. My parents told us to leave the house right away if we see or smell smoke.

2. Smoke can hurt you.

3. Because my sister is a little baby, my parents must help her.

4. My parents put her in the next bedroom.

5. It is up to us to make our homes safe from fire.

Think About It!

Set #5 Keeping Safe from Fire

In the sentences below, write on the line provided whether the <u>underlined</u> pronoun is a **subject pronoun** or an **object pronoun**.

Answers are on page 220.

Examples

Ms. Wu is teaching **<u>us</u>** about fire safety.   object pronoun

<u>She</u> wants us to be safe.   subject pronoun

<u>We</u> can be safe by following some simple rules.   subject pronoun

Let's learn about **them**.   object pronoun
They will make our lives safer.   subject pronoun

1. <u>We</u> should never play with matches. _____

2. Only adults should use <u>them</u>. _____

3. Matches can burn <u>you</u>. _____

4. <u>We</u> have smoke detectors in our house. _____

5. Smoke will cause <u>them</u> to make a loud sound. _____

 **Key Points!**

You can use a *pronoun* to take the place of a noun in a sentence.

A *subject pronoun* takes the place of the subject of the sentence.
Subject pronouns can be singular or plural.

<u>I</u> always go swimming with an adult.   (singular)
<u>He</u> is going swimming with us.   (singular)
<u>We</u> always go swimming with my father.   (plural)
<u>They</u> are swimming with an adult.   (plural)

An *object pronoun* takes the place of the object of the sentence.
Object pronouns can be singular or plural.

My uncle takes <u>me</u> swimming.   (singular)
I follow <u>him</u>.   (singular)
My uncle takes <u>us</u> swimming.   (plural)

POSSESSIVE PRONOUNS

Some **pronouns** can take the place of *possessive nouns*, which are nouns showing ownership. We call a **pronoun** taking the place of a possessive noun a **possessive pronoun**. Possessive pronouns can be singular or plural. The following table lists some **possessive pronouns**.

Singular	Plural
my	our
her	their
his	their
its	
your	

My class is learning about crossing a street safely.

A police officer visited **your** class.

Her name was Officer Wong.

Our city has many police officers to help keep us safe.

We owe them much respect.

Let's Try It!
Set #6 Crossing a Street

<u>Underline</u> the **possessive pronoun** from the two choices of **pronouns** in parentheses ( ) in each of the following sentences. Write your sentence on the line provided.

Answers are on page 220.

Examples

Ms. Wu talked to (my, me) class about safely crossing the street.
Ms. Wu talked to (<u>my</u>, me) class about safely crossing the street.

She told us (us, our) job is to wait for the crossing guard to tell us when to cross.
She told us (us, <u>our</u>) job is to wait for the crossing guard to tell us when to cross.

Mr. Alvarez is (he, his) name.
Mr. Alvarez is (he, <u>his</u>) name.

1. (My, Me) family lives on a street where a lot of cars drive.

    _____

2. (We, Our) parents walk to school with us every day.

    _____

3. Sometimes Papa drives us in (his, him) car.

    _____

4. He says (us, our) safety is very important to Mama and him.

    _____

5. (Your, You) school crossing guard can help you cross the street safely.

    _____

Think About It!

Set #7 Our School Crossing Guard

Unscramble the words to make a sentence. Write your sentence on the line provided. <u>Underline</u> the **possessive pronoun** in each sentence.

Answers are on page 220.

Examples

Mr. Alvarez school crossing our is guard.
<u>Mr. Alvarez is **our** school crossing guard.</u>

also He my is uncle
<u>He is also **my** uncle.</u>

My is very proud him of family
<u>**My** family is very proud of him.</u>

1. keeps He safe my friends

   _____

2. safety Our is important him to

   _____

3. street Our has many cars it on

   _____

4. drivers The stop cars their

   _____

5. crossing guard Your can you help

   _____

Key Points!

Possessive pronouns take the place of possessive nouns.

Juan's dog	<u>His</u> dog
Claudelle's book	<u>Her</u> book
Domingo's pencil	<u>My</u> pencil

Possessive pronouns may be either *singular* or *plural*.

<u>my</u> dog	<u>our</u> dog
<u>his</u> cat	<u>their</u> cat
<u>my</u> school	<u>their</u> school

Think About It!
Set #8 Getting Help Crossing the Street

<u>Underline</u> the different types of **pronouns** (*subject pronouns*, *object pronouns*, and *possessive pronouns*) in the sentences below.

Answers are on page 220.

Examples

<u>Our</u> mother watches <u>us</u> cross the street.

<u>My</u> sister and <u>I</u> look both ways before crossing a street.

<u>We</u> want to be safe when <u>we</u> cross the street.

1. We have to cross two streets on our way to school.

2. My brother walks with me to school.

3. He is in the sixth grade at our school.

4. He shows me how to look both ways before we cross the street.

5. I am glad I have a big brother who helps me cross the street.

56

Wrapping It Up!

A *pronoun* is a word that can take the place of a noun.

Safety is very important.   <u>It</u> is very important.
Luisa is my sister.   <u>She</u> is my sister.

A *subject pronoun* is a pronoun describing *who* or *what* the sentence is about.

<u>We</u> are learning to swim.   <u>I</u> like to swim.
<u>They</u> cross the street.   <u>He</u> crosses the street.

An *object pronoun* is a pronoun following an action verb and receives the action of the sentence

Mama told <u>us</u> not to play near the street.
Their school crossing guard helped <u>them</u> cross the street.

A *possessive pronoun* is a pronoun showing *ownership*. It can take the place of a possessive noun or nouns.

Juan's mother walked him across the busy street.
<u>His</u> mother walked them across the busy street.

Chapter 4

Putting Nouns and Pronouns into Action
A Chapter about Verbs

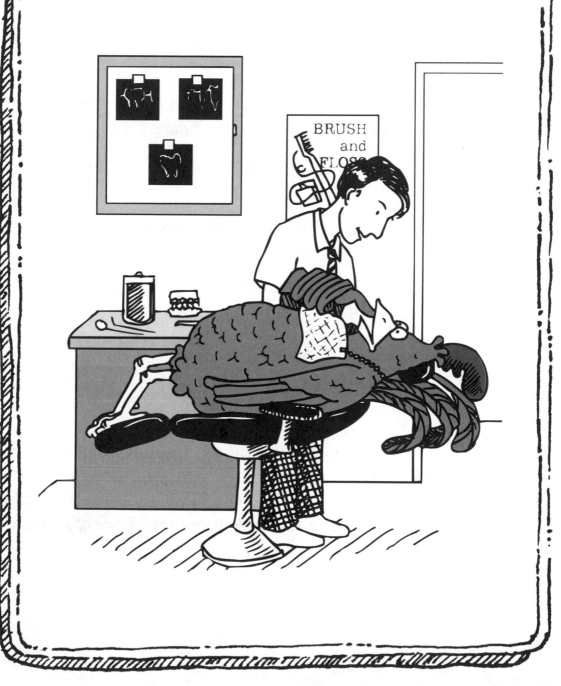

TERMS AND DEFINITIONS

Verb: A word telling what the subject of the sentence *is* or what it *is doing*.

Action Verb: A verb telling what the subject of the sentence *is doing*.

Linking Verb: A verb telling what the subject of the sentence *is*.

Verb Tense: Tells whether what is happening is in the *present*, in the *past*, or in the *future*.

Present Tense: The verb tense showing action *happening now*.

Past Tense: The verb tense showing action that has *already happened*.

Future Tense: The verb tense showing action that *will happen later*.

VERBS

In the first two chapters, you learned about *nouns* and *pronouns*. Now it is time to put those nouns and pronouns into action. **Verbs** do that! In this chapter, Shakespeare will help you to learn about **verbs** and how to use them, and at the same time talk about *taking care of your health*.

WHAT IS A VERB?

In Chapter 1, you learned that a sentence contains two main parts: a *subject* and a *predicate*. The *subject* tells you who or what the sentence is about. The *predicate* describes who or what the subject *is* or what the subject *is doing*. In the sentence below, the subject of the sentence is single-underlined, and the predicate is double-underlined. In every sentence, the **verb** is always in the predicate.

Juan **brushes** his teeth every morning and every night.

Lisa **visits** the dentist once a year.

ACTION VERBS

In the first example sentence you just read, the **verb** is *brushes*. It tells you what the subject *Juan* is doing. In the second example sentence, the **verb** is *visits*. It tells you what the subject *Lisa* does. We call these kinds of verbs that tell what the subject is doing **action verbs**. The following table lists some **action verbs**.

Action Verbs	
jump	run
walk	talk
write	read
look	help
teach	sing
skip	listen
learn	hide
kick	hit
dance	play
laugh	cry

We **walk** to school every morning.

I **dance** when I am happy.

I **help** my mother make dinner.

I **look** at the birds every morning.

We **laugh** at Ms. Wu's jokes.

Careful!

If you write a verb together with some other words, you may not have written a sentence! Make sure the group of words you have written has both a *subject* and a *predicate*.

Brushes his teeth   (This is not a sentence because there is no subject.)

Ugo brushes his teeth.   (This is a sentence because it has a subject and a predicate.)

Key Points!

Every sentence must contain a *subject* and a *predicate*.

The *subject* tells who or what the sentence is about.

The *predicate* describes who or what the subject *is* or what the subject *is doing*.

The <u>verb</u> is always in the *predicate*.

Let's Try It!
Set #1 A Trip to the Dentist

<u>Underline</u> the **action verb** in each of the following sentences.

Answers are on page 220.

Examples
I **<u>visited</u>** my dentist last week.
The dentist **<u>asked</u>** me about my teeth.
She **<u>taught</u>** me a lot about dental health.
I also **<u>learned</u>** about dental health in school.

1. My mother takes me to the dentist once a year.

2. My dentist asks me about my teeth.

3. She said too much candy and soft drinks are bad for my teeth.

4. The sugar in candy and soft drinks makes cavities in your teeth.

5. The dentist told me cavities are holes in your teeth.

Think About It!

Set #2 More about Dental Health

Now it's your turn to use **action verbs** to write about how *you take care of your teeth*. Choose from the **action verbs** listed below to write your sentences. Select the correct **action verb** and write your sentence on the line provided.

Answers are on page 221.

washes	helps	runs	want
drink	walks	sings	
jumps	enjoy	says	
eat	watches	flies	

Examples

I **want** to have clean, healthy teeth.

I **brush** my teeth after every meal.

1. I don't _____ a lot of candy because candy can cause cavities.

   _____

2. I also don't _____ a lot of soft drinks because soft drinks can cause cavities.

   _____

3. My little sister _____ me brush my teeth.

   _____

4. I _____ showing my little sister how to brush her teeth.

   _____

5. My mother _____ both of us will have clean, healthy teeth.

   _____

Key Points!

Action verbs tell your reader what the subject of the sentence *is doing*.

Using a variety of *action verbs* will make your writing more interesting because readers enjoy reading about action.

Try to learn some new *action verbs* each week. Write them in a notebook.

You can start your list with these *action verbs*: *throw*, *sing*, *play*, *read*, and *write*.

LINKING VERBS

Not all verbs are *action verbs*. Some verbs are **linking verbs**. **Linking verbs** tell what the subject of the sentence *is*. The **linking verb** most often used is a form of the verb **be**, such as *am, is, are, was, were*, and *will be*. Below are some examples of how **linking verbs** help you write sentences.

I **am** a second-grader.

I **will be** 8 years old next week.

My brother and I **are** twins.

We **were** first-graders last year.

Dr. Saldivar **is** my dentist.

Key Points!

Action verbs tell you what the subject of the sentence is *doing*.

       Dr. Saldivar <u>looks</u> at my teeth.
       Ms. Wu and Ms. Gonzalez <u>teach</u> us about being healthy.

Linking verbs tell you what the subject of the sentence *is*.

       Dr. Saldivar <u>is</u> my dentist.
       Ms. Wu and Ms. Gonzalez <u>are</u> our teachers.

The words *am, is, are, was, were,* and *will be* are *linking verbs*.

Let's Try It!

Set #3 Eating and Health

In each of the sentences below, <u>underline</u> the **linking verb**.

Answers are on page 221.

Examples

My friends Luis and Omar **are** in my homeroom.
I **am** in the third grade.
I **will be** in the fourth grade next year.
Ms. Wu **is** my teacher, and she teaches us about healthy eating.

1. Healthy eating is very important.

2. I am a healthy eater.

3. Ms. Wu is in good health because she eats lots of fruits and vegetables.

4. My sister was an unhealthy eater.

5. She will be healthy because now she eats foods that are good for her body.

SUBJECT–LINKING VERB AGREEMENT

When you write a **linking verb**, it must *agree* with the **subject**. That means, if the subject is *singular*, the **linking verb** must be *singular*. If the subject is *plural*, the linking verb must be *plural*.

I **am** 8 years old. (singular subject; singular linking verb)

We **are** second-graders. (plural subject; plural linking verb)

Ms. Garcia **is** my reading teacher. (singular subject; singular linking verb)

Ms. Garcia and *Mr. Obeyneke* **are** my favorite teachers. (plural subject; plural linking verb)

 **Key Points!**

A *linking verb* and its *subject* must *agree* with each other.

You must use a *singular linking verb* when you use a *singular subject*.

> *She* <u>is</u> my teacher.
> *Ms. Wu* <u>will be</u> my teacher.

You must use a *plural linking verb* when you use a *plural subject*.

> *They* <u>are</u> my brothers.
> *My brothers* <u>were</u> late.

Let's Try It!

Set #4 Healthy Foods

Complete each sentence by selecting the correct **linking verb** from the **linking verbs** in parentheses ( ). Write your sentence on the line provided.

Answers are on page 221.

Examples

Broccoli **is** one of many vegetables that are very good for you. (is, are)
Vegetables **are** good sources of vitamins and minerals. (is, are)
After eating a good breakfast, we **were** ready to go to school. (was, were)
Last year, Ms. Wu **was** our health teacher. (was, were)

1. Oranges and grapefruits _____ fruits. (is, are)

_____

2. Each piece of fruit I ate _____ delicious. (was, were)

_____

3. Oranges and grapefruits _____ good sources of Vitamin C. (is, are)

_____

4. Beans _____ a good source of vitamins and protein. (is, are)

_____

5. I _____ a healthy eater. (am, are)

_____

Careful!

Every sentence must have a *verb*. A *verb* can be either an *action verb* or a *linking verb*.

Think About It!
Set #5 Eating a Healthy Diet

<u>Underline</u> the **action verb** or the **linking verb** in each of the sentences below. On the line following the sentence, write the kind of **verb** you <u>underlined</u>.

Answers are on page 221.

Examples

My name **is** Rosa.   **Linking Verb**

I **eat** two pieces of fruit every day.   **Action Verb**

I **am** a student at Cortez Elementary School.   **Linking Verb**

My class **learned** that fruits and vegetables are good for us. **Action Verb**

1. My mother serves us vegetables with dinner. _____

2. Broccoli and spinach are my favorite vegetables. _____

3. "Junk food" provides little nutrition for your body. _____

4. Doughnuts and cupcakes are examples of junk food. _____

5. Healthy food is good for your body. _____

 **Key Points!**

Linking verbs are important words because they tell the reader who or what the subject of the sentence *is*.

Use *linking verbs* when you need to, but also remember to use *action verbs* more often.

Action verbs make your writing more interesting because readers enjoy reading about action.

VERB TENSES

The *tense* of a verb tells whether what is happening takes place in the *present*, in the *past*, or in the *future*.

PRESENT TENSE VERBS

The **present tense** shows action <u>happening now</u>. Usually, you write a verb in the present tense by adding **-s** or **-es** to the base verb when the subject is *singular*.

Mario **plays** soccer every day after school.

Ms. Wu **teaches** us that daily exercise, like playing soccer, is good for you.

Jorge **enjoys** playing baseball with his friends.

The table below lists some **present tense** verbs.

Some Present Tense Verbs		
hops	helps	plays
improves	enjoys	smiles
walks	looks	jumps
crawls	skips	laughs
says	cheers	catches

Let's Try It!
Set # 6 Playing Outside Is Good Exercise

From the list below, choose **verbs** in the **present tense** to complete each sentence. Write your sentence on the line provided.

Answers are on page 221.

think   like   says   plays   cheers   hits   catches   kicks

Examples

Jorge **plays** outside with his friends.

He **hits** the ball with his bat.

Isis **catches** the ball.

1. Maria _____ the soccer ball into the goal.

_____

2. Her friend _____ when the ball flies into the goal.

_____

3. "I _____ to play soccer," says Maria.

_____

4. My mother _____ playing soccer is good exercise.

_____

5. I _____ exercise is fun!

_____

Past Tense Verbs

The **past tense** shows action that has <u>already happened</u>. You can write most verbs in the **past tense** by adding **-d** or **-ed** to the end of the base verb.

Last summer, I **played** baseball.

Last year, I **walked** to school every day.

I **enjoyed** the outdoors and spending time with my friends.

Playing outdoors **improved** my health.

The following table lists some **past tense** verbs.

Some Past Tense Verbs		
hopped	helped	played
improved	enjoyed	smiled
walked	looked	jumped
crawled	skipped	laughed
raced	scored	talked

Let's Try It!
Set #7 Fun Things That Help Us Exercise
<u>Underline</u> the **past tense verb** in each of the sentences.

Answers are on page 221.

Examples
Ugo and I **played** basketball yesterday.
Ugo **scored** two baskets.
Last week, we **raced** up and down the soccer field.

1. I played outside for 15 minutes yesterday.

2. Ellie skipped to her apartment.

3. I jumped into a swimming pool last Saturday.

4. My little sister waded in the water at the shallow end.

5. Mama smiled at my little sister.

FUTURE TENSE VERBS

The **future tense** shows action that will <u>happen later</u>. When you write in the **future tense**, you usually write the word *will* or *shall* in front of the base verb. Use *shall* when you have to or intend to do something. Use *will* when you are not as sure about your action.

I **<u>will try</u>** to play outside more.

Exercise **<u>will help</u>** me to stay healthy.

My parents said they **<u>will exercise</u>** with me.

I **<u>shall exercise</u>** every day.

The table below lists some **future tense** verbs.

Some Future Tense Verbs		
will hop	shall help	will play
shall improve	will enjoy	will smile
will walk	shall look	will jump
will crawl	will skip	will laugh
shall help	shall study	will learn

Let's Try It!
Set #8 Keeping Myself Healthy

Unscramble the words on each line to write a sentence. Write your sentence on the line provided. <u>Underline</u> the **future tense verb** in each of your sentences.

Answers are on page 222.

Examples

health Good help will you life enjoy
Good health **will help** you enjoy life.

be healthy try I will to
I **will try** to be healthy.

do will by eating that healthy I
I **will do** that by eating healthy.

1. will exercise day every I

_____

2. outside play friends with my I will

_____

3. My will cook food mother good

_____

4. shall fruits I eat and vegetables

_____

5. junk food avoid I will

_____

Key Points!

The *present tense* shows action <u>happening now</u>.

    I <u>play</u> soccer.   I <u>do</u> my homework.

The *past tense* shows action that <u>already happened</u>.

    I <u>played</u> soccer.   I <u>finished</u> my homework.

The *future tense* shows action that <u>will happen</u>.

    I <u>will play</u> soccer.   I <u>will do</u> my homework.

Careful!

Make sure all the *verbs* you use in a sentence are in the correct *tense*.

Incorrect:

Yesterday, Obi *run* and *skip* to school.

The *verbs* in this sentence should be written in the *past tense* because we are talking about something Obi did <u>yesterday</u>.

Correct:

Yesterday, Obi *ran* and *skipped* to school.

Let's Try It!
Set #9 Exercise for Good Health

For each sentence below, underline the **verb**. On the blank line following each sentence, write the **verb tense** (*present tense*, *past tense*, or *future tense*) the **verb** is written in.

Answers are on page 222.

Examples

My father <u>exercises</u> every day.   **Present Tense**

Last week, he <u>ran</u> 2 miles every day.   **Past Tense**

Running <u>will help</u> him become more physically fit.   **Future Tense**

1. I walk to school every day.   _____

2. My mother says that walking is good exercise for her and me.   _____

3. Next year, my little brother will walk with us.   _____

4. My sister played outside yesterday.   _____

5. Good health makes your life fun!   _____

The table below lists some **verbs** in the *present tense*, *past tense*, and the *future tense*.

Present Tense	Past Tense	Future Tense
hops	hopped	will hop
helps	helped	shall help
plays	played	will play
improves	improved	shall improve
enjoys	enjoyed	will enjoy
smiles	smiled	will smile
walks	walked	will walk
looks	looked	shall look
jumps	jumped	will jump
crawls	crawled	will crawl
skips	skipped	will skip
laughs	laughed	will laugh

Think About It!
Set #10 Visiting the Doctor

For each sentence below, <u>underline</u> the correct **verb** that completes the sentence in the **verb tense** written in parentheses ( ). Write your sentence on the line provided.

Answers are on page 222.

Examples

I (visit, **visited**) my doctor yesterday.   **(Past Tense)**
My parents (**take**, took) us to the doctor every year.   **(Present Tense)**
We (**will go**, went) again next year.   **(Future Tense)**

1. My doctor (examined, examines) my hearing and breathing. (Past Tense)

   _____

2. I (heard, hear) and breathe well. (Present Tense)

   _____

3. Next year at school, I (will read, read) an eye chart to check my eyesight. (Future Tense)

   _____

4. A doctor's examination (helps, helped) prevent health problems. (Present Tense)

   _____

5. I (will visit, visited) my doctor next September. (Future Tense)

   _____

Wrapping It Up!

A *verb* is a word telling what the subject of the sentence <u>is</u> or what it <u>is doing</u>.

My mother <u>is</u> a good cook.
She <u>feeds</u> me healthy foods.

An *action verb* is a verb telling what the subject of the sentence is <u>doing</u>.

I <u>play</u> outside every day.   I <u>enjoy</u> the outdoors.

A *linking verb* is a verb telling what the subject of the sentence <u>is</u>.

My father <u>is</u> a mechanic.   I <u>am</u> a second-grader.

A *linking verb* and its *subject* must *agree*.

Use a singular linking verb with a singular subject.
My <u>mother</u> *is* Asian.

Use a plural linking verb with a plural subject.
My <u>uncles</u> *are* African.

A *verb's tense* tells whether the action takes place in the *present*, in the *past*, or in the *future*.

The *present tense* shows action that is <u>happening now</u>.

I <u>walk</u> to school.   I <u>play</u> with my friends.

The *past tense* shows action that has <u>already happened.</u>

I <u>walked</u> to school.   I <u>played</u> with my friends.

The *future tense* shows action that <u>will happen later</u>.

I <u>shall walk</u> to school.   I <u>will play</u> with my friends.

Chapter 5

How Do You Describe and Compare?

A Chapter about Adjectives and Adverbs

TERMS AND DEFINITIONS

Adjective: A word telling your reader more about the *noun* or *pronoun* in the sentence.

Article: The words *a*, *an*, and *the*.

Adverb: Words describing or telling your reader more about *verbs*, *adjectives,* or other *adverbs* in the sentence.

ADJECTIVES AND ADVERBS

Adjectives and **adverbs** are also called *describing* words. They tell your reader more about the nouns, pronouns, and other words in your writing. By doing this, they make your writing clearer and more interesting. By learning to use **adjectives** and **adverbs**, you will become a better writer. So let's get started!

Shakespeare is here to help. While he helps you write with **adjectives** and **adverbs**, he will also tell you some interesting things about *our planet Earth*, the *other planets in our solar system,* and *the stars*.

WHAT IS AN ADJECTIVE?

An **adjective** is a word telling your reader more about the *noun* or *pronoun* in the sentence.

DESCRIBING WITH ADJECTIVES

Adjectives can help you *describe* people, places, and things. The following are some of the ways **adjectives** can *describe* things.

How many things we have.

An orbit is **one** trip around the sun. (How many *trips?*)
Mars has **two** moons. (How many *moons?*)
Saturn has **many** rings. (How many *rings?*)

What **color** something is.

I am wearing **black** shoes. (What color *shoes?*)
Mars is a **red** planet. (What color *planet?*)
Earth has **blue** oceans. (What color *oceans?*)

How something **sounds**.

Miguel talks in a **loud** voice. (How does *Miguel's voice* sound?)
Ms. Wu has a **soft** voice. (How does *Ms. Vu's voice* sound?)
The bird has a **shrill** call. (How does the *bird's call* sound?)

How something **tastes**.

I like **sweet** apples. (How do the *apples* taste?)
Obi likes to eat **sour** lemons. (How do the *lemons* taste?)
I like **spicy** salsa. (How does the *salsa* taste?)

How something **looks**.

Alicia is a **beautiful** baby.   (How does the *baby* look?)
Romero is holding an **ugly** toad.   (How does the *toad* look?)
Obi is a **handsome** boy.   (How does the *boy* look?)

How something **feels**.

Isis is holding a **smooth** rock.   (How does the *rock* feel?)
I lay my head on a **soft** pillow.   (How does the *pillow* feel?)
I am holding a **rough** piece of wood.   (How does the *wood* feel?)

What **size** something is.

Our sun is a **large** star!   (What is the size of the *star*?)
Mercury is a **small** planet.   (What is the size of the *planet*?)

ADJECTIVES YOU CAN USE TO DESCRIBE

Using **adjectives** will improve your writing by making it more
interesting, because when you *describe* someone or something well to
your reader, it becomes more interesting for them to read about. The
table below lists some **adjectives** *describing* people, places, and things.
You can use these in your writing. Try to learn a few more adjectives
each week and write them in your notebook.

Adjectives You Can Use to Describe		
small	large	tall
short	happy	sad
round	square	rough
smooth	soft	hard

red	blue	green
sour	spicy	salty
hot	cold	warm
rich	poor	high
low	angry	mad

Careful!

Numbers can be *adjectives* too.

fifteen cookies   *twenty* students
thirty books

Mom baked *fifteen* cookies.
Ms. Wu has *twenty* students in her class.
Dr. Montoya read *thirty* books last summer.

Let's Try It!
Set #1 Our Solar System

<u>Underline</u> the **adjective** showing **how many** of something there are in each of the sentences below.

Answers are on page 222.

Examples
There are <u>**eight**</u> planets in our solar system: Mercury, Venus, Earth, Mars, Jupiter, Saturn, Uranus, and Neptune.
Our solar system has <u>**one**</u> star: the sun.
Some planets have <u>**many**</u> moons revolving around them.

1. Earth has one moon.

2. Jupiter has many moons.

85

3. The time it takes a planet to orbit around the sun is 1 year.

4. There are 365 days in a year if you live on Earth.

5. If you lived on Mercury, your year would have 88 days.

 **Key Points!**

Adjectives can help you *describe* <u>persons</u>, <u>places</u>, and <u>things</u>.

Adjectives can *describe* by telling you the following things:

number	<u>two</u> moons
color	<u>red</u> planet
sound	<u>loud</u> voice
taste	<u>sour</u> apple
look	<u>beautiful</u> sky
feel	<u>smooth</u> stone
size	<u>large</u> planet

COMPARING WITH REGULAR ADJECTIVES

You can also use an **adjective** to *compare* things. By *comparing* one thing to something else, you provide your reader with information that makes your writing more interesting.

Most **adjectives** are **regular adjectives**. When using **regular adjectives**, you add *-er* to the base adjective to <u>compare two nouns</u>. **Adjectives** with an *-er* ending are often used before the word *than*.

Earth is **larger** *than* Mercury.
Venus is **hotter** *than* Earth.
Saturn is **farther** from the sun *than* Earth is.

You use **regular adjectives** ending with *-est* to <u>compare three or more nouns</u>. **Adjectives** with an *-est* ending are often used after the word *the*.

Jupiter is *the* **largest** planet in our solar system.
Venus is *the* **hottest** planet in our solar system.
Mercury has *the* **shortest** orbit of all the planets.

Careful!

Before adding the *-er* or *-est* ending to some adjectives, you may have to <u>double the final consonant</u>. Check a dictionary or ask your teacher if you are not sure.

hot	hotter, hottest
big	bigger, biggest
fat	fatter, fattest
slim	slimmer, slimmest

Yesterday was a <u>**hot**</u> day.
Today is <u>**hotter**</u> *than* yesterday.
Tomorrow will be *the* <u>**hottest**</u> day.

Rex is a **fat** dog.
Shep is a **fatter** dog *than* Rex.
Spot is *the* **fattest** dog.

Careful!

Before adding the *-er* or *-est* ending to adjectives ending in
-y, you have to change the ending *-y* to *-i*.

skinny	skinnier, skinniest
funny	funnier, funniest
happy	happier, happiest

Regina has a **happy** laugh.
Isis has a **happier** laugh *than* Regina.
Claudelle has *the* **happiest** laugh of the three girls.

Obi made a **funny** face.
Alexander made a **funnier** face *than* Obi.
Nicholas made *the* **funniest** face of all.

Let's Try It!
Set #2 Our Solar System: The Biggest and the Fastest

In each of the sentences below, select and <u>underline</u> the correct *comparing* adjective.

Answers are on page 222.

Examples

Jupiter is the (bigger, **biggest**) planet in our solar system.
Mercury is the (**smallest**, small) planet in our solar system.
Earth is (biggest, **bigger**) than Mercury.

1. Mercury has the (fastest, fast) orbit of any planet in our solar system.

2. Of all the planets, Mercury is the (closer, closest) to the sun.

3. Earth is (close, closer) to the sun than Jupiter.

4. That means Earth has a (shortest, shorter) year than Jupiter.

5. Neptune has the (longer, longest) year of all the planets.

ADJECTIVES YOU CAN USE TO COMPARE

The earlier table listed some **adjectives** you can use to *describe* people and places. The table below lists some **adjectives** *comparing* people and places. Try to learn a few new **adjectives** each week and write them in your special notebook.

Adjectives You Can Use to *Compare*		
small	smaller	smallest
large	larger	largest

tall	taller	tallest
short	shorter	shortest
happy	happier	happiest
sad	sadder	saddest
round	rounder	roundest
rough	rougher	roughest
hot	hotter	hottest
cold	colder	coldest
warm	warmer	warmest
bold	bolder	boldest
near	nearer	nearest

Think About It!
Set #3 Earth's Neighbors

Select the correct **adjective** that *compares* in each sentence. Write your new sentence on the line provided.

Answers are on page 222.

Examples

Of all the planets in our solar system, Venus is the (near, nearer, **nearest**) to Earth.

Venus is (near, **nearer**, nearest) to the sun than Earth.

1. Venus is (hot, hotter, hottest) than Earth.

_____

2. Jupiter is (large, larger, largest) than Earth.

_____

3. Jupiter is the (large, larger, largest) of the planets in our solar system.

_____

4. Mars has a (long, longer, longest) year than Earth.

_____

5. Earth is (close, closer, closest) to the sun than Mars.

_____

 **Key Points!**

An _adjective_ can be used to <u>compare</u> things.

Most adjectives are _regular adjectives_.

When using _regular adjectives_, you add _-er_ to the base adjective when comparing two nouns. _Adjectives_ with an _-er_ ending are often used before the word _than_.

> Venus is <u>hotter</u> _than_ Earth.
> Jupiter is <u>larger</u> _than_ Neptune.

When using _regular adjectives_, you add _-est_ to the base adjective when comparing three or more nouns. _Adjectives_ with an _-est_ ending are often used after the word _the_.

> Jupiter is _the_ <u>largest</u> of all the planets.
> Mercury is _the_ <u>closest</u> planet to the sun.

COMPARING WITH IRREGULAR ADJECTIVES

COMPARING WITH *GOOD* AND *BAD*

The adjectives *good* and *bad* are **adjectives** writers often use. Each word takes a special form when it is comparing nouns. These special types of adjectives are called **irregular adjectives** because they do not form their comparing words in the regular way by adding *-er* and *-est*.

First, let's look at the adjective *good*. Notice that the adjective **good** completely changes its form when it *compares* nouns.

Using the Irregular Adjective *Good*

Base Adjective	Comparing Two Nouns	Comparing Three or More Nouns
good	better	best

Notice how the word *than* is used when you use the adjective **better**. When you use the adjective **best**, write the word *the* before the adjective in the sentence.

Mario has a **good** telescope for looking at the planets.
Mario has a **better** telescope *than* I do for looking at the planets.
Mario has *the* **best** telescope of all for looking at the planets.

I have a **good** view of the planet Mars.
I have a **better** view of the planet Mars *than* Isis does.
Of all of us, I have *the* **best** view of the planet Mars.

Let's Try It!

Set #4 Astronomy: The Study of the Stars and Planets

Select, and write on the line provided, the correct **adjective** (*good*, *better*, or *best*) to complete each sentence below.

Answers are on page 223.

Examples

I read a **good** book about the stars and planets.
She has a **better** telescope than Mr. Chin.
When it comes to teaching us astronomy, Ms. Wu is the **best** teacher.

1. Of all the planets, I like the planet Jupiter the _____.

2. I enjoy learning about Earth _____ than learning about Jupiter.

3. I am _____ at locating Mars with my telescope.

4. Of everyone in the classroom, Ms. Wu is the _____ user of the telescope.

5. I read a _____ book about astronomy than Juan read.

Now let's see how to use the adjective *bad* to compare nouns. Notice that it takes a special form when it *compares* nouns. The following table shows the special forms.

Using the Irregular Adjective *Bad*

Base Adjective	Comparing Two Nouns	Comparing Three or More Nouns
bad	worse	worst

Notice how the writer uses the word *than* when the adjective **worse** is used. Similarly, you should write the word *the* before the adjective **worst** in the sentence.

My sister said she had a **bad** day.
My brother said his day was **worse** *than* hers.
I had *the* **worst** day of all.

Jenna had a **bad** cut on her finger.
Marcy had a **worse** cut *than* Jenna.
Ramona had *the* **worst** cut of all.

Let's Try It!
Set #5 Bad Weather on Earth and Elsewhere

Select the correct **adjective** (*bad*, *worse,* or *worst*) to complete each sentence below. Write your sentence on the line provided.

Answers are on page 223.

Examples
School was closed yesterday because we had **bad** weather.
Today's weather might be **worse** *than* yesterday's weather.
Yesterday was *the* **worst** day of my life!

1. We had some _____ weather yesterday.

   _____

2. The weather was _____ on Monday than yesterday.

   _____

3. The _____ weather of all is yet to come!

   _____

4. Planets also have _____ weather.

   _____

5. Of the planets Earth, Mercury, and Mars, Mars has the _____ weather.

   _____

COMPARING WITH *MANY* AND *LITTLE*

There aren't nearly as many **irregular adjectives** as regular adjectives, but some irregular adjectives are frequently used. Let's look at two more commonly used **irregular adjectives**: *many* and *little*.

Comparing with *Many* and *Little*

Base Adjective	Comparing Two Nouns	Comparing Three or More Nouns
many	more	most
little	less	least

Notice how the word *than* is written in sentences where you are *comparing two nouns*. When you compare *three or more nouns*, you write the word *the* before the adjective.

Some planets in our solar system have **many** moons.
Mars has **more** moons *than* Earth.
Jupiter has *the* **most** moons of any planet.

I spent a **little** time looking through the telescope.
I spent **less** time looking through the telescope *than* you did.
Tony spent *the* **least** time looking through the telescope.

Think About It!
Set #6 Using *Many* and *Little*

Unscramble the words on each line to make a sentence. Write your sentence on the line provided. Notice how each sentence uses a form of the **irregular adjectives** *many* or *little*.

Answers are on page 223.

Examples
Ramona spent the studying for the test **most** time
Ramona spent *the* **most** time studying for the test.

Alexis spent **more** than time Juan for the test studying
Alexis spent **more** time *than* Juan studying for the test.

1. a **little** spent I time playing outside

_____

2. Joanna the **least** spent time outside playing

_____

3. Hector spent **most** the time playing outside

_____

4. I **less** ate than Roberto.

_____

5. Roberto **more** ate than ate I

_____

COMPARING WITH _BEAUTIFUL_ AND _CAREFUL_

Some **irregular adjectives** compare by adding the words _more, most, less,_ and _least_ in front of them. Two commonly used **irregular adjectives** that do this are the **irregular adjectives** _beautiful_ and _careful_.

Comparing with _Beautiful_ and _Careful_

Base Adjective	Comparing Two Nouns	Comparing Three or More Nouns
beautiful	more beautiful	most beautiful
beautiful	less beautiful	least beautiful
careful	more careful	most careful
careful	less careful	least careful

Notice that the word *than* appears in sentences *comparing two nouns.* By comparison, notice that the word *the* appears in sentences *comparing three or more nouns.*

Yesterday, we saw a **beautiful** sunset.
I think tonight's sunset is **more beautiful** *than* yesterday's sunset.
Last Thursday's sunset was *the* **most beautiful** of the three sunsets.

I am **careful** when I use the telescope.
Juan is **more careful** *than* Oscar when he uses the telescope.
Naomi is *the* **least careful** of the three of us.

Think About It!
Set #7 Looking at the Stars

Choose from the **irregular adjectives** listed below to complete the sentences. Write your sentence on the line provided.

Answers are on page 223.

beautiful	more beautiful	most beautiful
careful	less careful	least careful
many	more	most
little	less	least

Examples
"The stars in the sky are **beautiful**," said Armando.
"This is the **most** stars I have ever seen!" exclaimed Carlos.

"I have seen **more** stars than this," Isis said.
A sky full of stars is **more beautiful** than a cloudy sky.

1. Sometimes when it is a _____ cloudy, it is hard to see the stars.

   _____

2. I am _____ when I look through someone's telescope.

   _____

3. You can see _____ stars when you are out in the country than when you are in the city.

   _____

4. You see more stars because there is _____ reflected light in the country than in the city. Reflected light makes it hard to see the stars.

   _____

   _____

5. I think a sky full of stars is the _____ sight of all!

   _____

Key Points!

Irregular adjectives change their forms when they compare nouns.

| good | better | best |
| bad | worse | worst |

many	more	most
little	less	least
beautiful	less, more beautiful	least, most beautiful
careful	less, more careful	least, most careful

Careful!

Improving your vocabulary by learning new *adjectives* is a good thing to do but remember to learn also whether the *adjective* is a <u>regular</u> <u>adjective</u> or an <u>irregular adjective</u>.

ARTICLES

The words *a*, *an*, and ***the*** are special **adjectives** called **articles**.

The **article *an*** is used before words beginning with a *vowel*.
Remember: The *vowels* in the English alphabet are the following letters: *a, e, i, o,* and *u.*

<u>**An**</u> astronomer is a person who studies the stars and planets. One planet's trip around the sun or a planet is called <u>**an**</u> orbit. <u>**An**</u> elephant would weigh less on the moon than on Earth because there is less gravity on the moon.

The **article *a*** is used before words beginning with a *consonant*.

Remember: Letters that are not *vowels* are *consonants.*

Earth is <u>a</u> planet.
<u>A</u> year is the time it takes for a planet to orbit the sun.
Earth is orbited by <u>a</u> moon.

The **article** *the* can be used before any word regardless of whether the word begins with a *vowel* or a *consonant*.

<u>The</u> astronomer looks through <u>the</u> telescope.
Venus is nearly the same size as <u>the</u> earth.
<u>The</u> rings around Saturn are made of rocks and gases.
<u>The</u> sky is full of stars.

Let's Try It!
Set #8 Our Sun

<u>Underline</u> the correct **article** or **articles** (*a*, *an*, or *the*) in each of the sentences below. Write your sentence on the line provided.

Answers are on page 223.

Examples
Our sun is (<u>a</u>, an) star.
(<u>A</u>, An) planet is different from (<u>a</u>, an) star.
(<u>The</u>, A) sun is the only star in our solar system.

1. (A, An) star is a ball of burning gas.

   _____

2. (The, An) gas is burning and is very hot.

   _____

3. Earth gets its light and heat from (an, the) sun.

   _____

4. (An, A) orbit around (an, the) sun takes 1 year.

_____

5. All (the, an) planets in our solar system orbit our sun.

_____

 Key Points!

The articles _a_, _an_, and _the_ are special adjectives called _articles_.

The article _a_ is used before words beginning with a _consonant_.

    _a_ planet   _a_ moon   _a_ telescope

The article _an_ is used before words beginning with a _vowel_.

    _an_ astronomer   _an_ orbit

The article _the_ can be used before any word.

    the planet   _the_ moon   _the_ orbit

ADVERBS

Now that you have learned to _describe_ and _compare_ nouns and pronouns with adjectives, let's learn how to _describe_ and _compare_ other parts of speech. To do that, you need to learn about **adverbs.**

WHAT IS AN ADVERB?

An **adverb** is a word that modifies a *verb*, an *adjective,* or another *adverb*. As you can see, you can use **adverbs** to *describe* and *compare* many different words! Let's see how to use them in your writing.

DESCRIBING AND COMPARING WITH ADVERBS

Using **adverbs** will improve your writing because you will be telling more to your reader about *verbs*, *adjectives*, and other *adverbs* that you are using in your writing.

Mercury *orbits* around the sun **quickly**.
The **adverb quickly** tells more about the **verb** *orbits*.

Jupiter is a **much** *larger* planet than Earth.
The **adverb much** tells more about the **adjective** *larger*.

The sun is **extremely** *hot*.
The **adverb extremely** tells more about the **adjective** *hot*.

Mercury orbits around the sun **very** *quickly*.
The **adverb very** tells more about the **adverb** *quickly*.

Let's Try It!
Set #9 *Describing* **and** *Comparing* **the Planets**

For each of the sentences below, underline the **adverb** and double-underline the **adjective** that the **adverb** is *describing* or *comparing*.

Answers are on page 224.

Examples

Mercury is **much** **closer** to the sun than Jupiter.

Saturn and Jupiter are **very** **large** planets.

Jupiter is an **extremely** **cold** planet.

1. Jupiter has many more moons than Earth.

2. It takes Jupiter and Saturn a very long time to orbit the sun.

3. Venus is an extremely hot planet.

4. Neptune is a very cold planet.

5. Venus is much closer to the sun than Neptune.

Think About It!

Set #10 More about the Planets

Unscramble the words and write your sentence on the line provided. Underline the **adverb** in each of the sentences you have written.

Answers are on page 224.

Examples

moon Earth's large craters many has

Earth's moon has **many** large craters.

Venus is very a hot planet

Venus is a **very** hot planet.

1. Earth very water much has in its oceans.

     _____

2. a big very planet Jupiter is

     _____

3. Uranus far extremely from sun the is

_____

4. close Mercury very is to the sun

_____

5. Mercury is closer much to Earth sun than is

_____

 **Key Points!**

An <u>adverb</u> tells more about a _verb_, an _adjective_, or another _adverb_.

> The clouds _slowly_ drifted through the sky.
> The sun is _much_ larger than Earth.
> The astronomer observes the planets _very_ carefully.

CHANGING ADJECTIVES TO ADVERBS

Remember **adjectives** describe and compare _nouns_ and _pronouns_. Some **adjectives** can be changed to **adverbs** by simply adding _-ly_ to the end of the **adjective**.

Below are some **adjectives** changed to **adverbs** by adding the ending _-ly_ to the **adjective**. Notice these **adverbs** describe _how_.

Adjective	Adverb
slow	slowly
sudden	suddenly
quick	quickly
close	closely
extreme	extremely
careful	carefully

Juan is a **slow** runner.
Slow is an **adjective** describing the **noun** *runner*.

Juan runs **slowly**.
Slowly is an **adverb** describing the **verb** *runs*.
How does Juan run? *slowly*

Obi is a **careful** reader.
Careful is an **adjective** describing the **noun** *reader*.

Obi reads **carefully**.
Carefully is an **adverb** describing the **verb** *reads*.
How does Obi read? *carefully*

Careful!

A sentence can have <u>more than one</u> *adverb*.

Juan ran **very carefully**.
Jenna read **more quickly**.

An *adverb* can be written <u>before</u> or <u>after</u> the verb.

> Juan **carefully** *ran* over the bumpy ground.
> Juan *ran* **carefully** over the bumpy ground.

An *adverb* can be written at the <u>beginning</u> or <u>end</u> of a sentence.

> **Carefully**, Juan *ran* over the bumpy ground.
> Juan *ran* over the bumpy ground **carefully**.

ADJECTIVES ENDING IN -Y

To change *adjectives* ending in -y into *adverbs*, follow these three easy steps:

1. To write an *adverb,* drop the ending -y in the *adjective*, then

2. add -i, and finally,

3. add -ly to the end of the word.

Adjective	Adverb
easy	easily
happy	happily
noisy	noisily

Obi **easily** *ran* the length of the soccer field.
I **happily** *blew* out the candles on my birthday cake.
Isis **noisily** *sat* down in her seat.

Let's Try It!
Set #11 Looking at the Sun and Planets

Select the correct **adjective** or **adverb** to complete the sentence. Write the sentence on the line provided.

Answers are on page 224.

Remember: Adjectives describe *nouns* and *pronouns*. **Adverbs** describe *verbs*, *adjectives*, and other *adverbs*.

Examples

Earth orbits (quick, quickly) around the sun.
Earth orbits **quickly** around the sun.

The *adverb* **quickly** describes the *verb* **orbit**.

The sun is a (bright, brightly) star.
The sun is a **bright** star.

The *adjective* **bright** describes the *noun* **star**.

1. Jupiter is a very (large, largely) planet.

   _____

2. The sun shines (bright, brightly) in the sky.

   _____

3. The sun shines (dim, dimly) in Neptune's sky because Neptune is far from the sun.

   _____

4. A telescope allows you to look (close, closely) at the planets.

   _____

Wrapping It Up!

An *adjective* is a word telling your reader more about a <u>noun</u> or <u>pronoun</u> in a sentence.

large planet   *many* rings   *fast* orbit

Articles are special adjectives. The words *a*, *an*, and *the* are *articles*.

The article *a* is used before a word beginning with a *consonant*.

a planet   *a* moon

The article *an* is used before a word beginning with a *vowel*.

an orbit   *an* astronomer

The article *the* can be used before a word beginning with either a *vowel* or a *consonant*.

the planet   *the* astronomer

An *adverb* is a word telling your reader more about <u>verbs</u>, <u>adjectives</u>, or other <u>adverbs</u> in the sentence.

quickly <u>orbited</u> *very* <u>big</u> planet *very* <u>carefully</u> walked

Chapter 6

Which Words Act Like Glue?
A Chapter about Prepositions and Conjunctions

TERMS AND DEFINITIONS

Preposition: A word showing how one noun or pronoun is related to another noun or pronoun in a sentence. A **preposition** helps *connect* the two nouns or pronouns.

Prepositional Phrase: A group of words beginning with a *preposition* and ending with a noun or pronoun.

Object of the Preposition: The noun or pronoun at the end of a *prepositional phrase*.

Conjunction: A word that *connects* words.

PREPOSITIONS

In the first five chapters, you learned about **nouns**, **pronouns**, **verbs**, **adjectives**, and **adverbs**. You also learned the job of each of these parts of speech and how important they are to good writing.

In this chapter, you will learn something else to help you write well. Most of the time, you need to have words to **connect** or **glue** other words together to make a sentence. This is where **prepositions** and **conjunctions** come in and help you. You can use these parts of speech to **connect** or **glue** your words together to write sentences, paragraphs, and stories.

So let's get started and see how these words can help your writing!

Once again, our friend Shakespeare is going to help us learn. This time, while he is helping you learn about **prepositions** and **conjunctions**, he will also be telling you some *interesting science facts*.

WHAT IS A PREPOSITION?

A **preposition** is a word showing how <u>one noun or pronoun</u> is **related** to <u>another noun or pronoun</u> in a sentence. The following table lists some **prepositions** you can use.

Some Useful Prepositions				
about	during	behind	below	by
for	in	on	off	under
across	beside	between	before	of
like	over	out	to	upon
at	up	onto	down	into

The book is **on** the desk.
On is a **preposition**.
The **preposition on** tells the reader how the *book* is **related** to the *desk*. It is **on** it.

Carla fell *off* her bicycle.
Off is a **preposition**.
The **preposition *off*** tells the reader
how *Carla* is **related** to her *bicycle*.
She is *off* it.

Pham hid *behind* the post.
Behind is a **preposition**.
The **preposition *behind*** tells the
reader how Pham is **related** to the
post. He is *behind* it.

Let's Try It!
Set #1 Weather and Climate

<u>Underline</u> the **preposition** or **prepositions** in each of the
sentences below. Use the table at the beginning of this
chapter to help you.

Answers are on page 224.

Examples
Weather is <u>**around**</u> us.
We experience weather all <u>**of**</u> the time.
Weather is the day-to-day conditions <u>**of**</u> a particular place.

1. *Climate* is the weather conditions over a long period.

2. We learned there is a difference between *weather* and *climate*.

3. Rain was forecast for today's *weather*.

4. The *climate* in our part of the country is hot and dry.

5. What is the *climate* of the region where you live?

PREPOSITIONAL PHRASES

A **prepositional phrase** is a group of words beginning with a **preposition** and ending with a *noun* or *pronoun*. We call the *noun* or *pronoun* at the end of a **prepositional phrase** the **object of the preposition**.

over the bridge   under the table   of the area

USING PREPOSITIONAL PHRASES

Propositional phrases show the *relationship* between the **subject** of the sentence and the **object**. In other words, the **prepositional phrase** *connects* the two words.

The car drove **over** the *bridge*.
Over is a **preposition**.
Bridge is the **object of the preposition**.
Over shows how the *car* is *related* to the *bridge*.

The cat hid **under** the *table*.
Under is the **preposition**. *Table* is the **object of the preposition**.
Under shows how the *cat* is *related* to the *table*.

The climate **of** the *area* is cold and damp.
Of is the **preposition**. *Area* is the **object** of the **preposition**.
Of shows how the *climate* is *related* to the *area*.

Key Points!

A *preposition* is a word showing how one noun or pronoun is *related* to another noun or pronoun in a sentence. A *preposition* helps to <u>connect</u> the two nouns or pronouns. For example,

   of   *under*   *over*

A *prepositional phrase* is a group of words beginning with a *preposition* and ending with a *noun* or *pronoun*.

   of the area   *under the table*   *over the bridge*

The *object of the preposition* is the *noun* or *pronoun* that ends the *prepositional phrase*.

   of the *area*   under the *table*   over the *bridge*

Let's Try It!
Set #2 The Human Skeleton

<u>Underline</u> the **prepositional phrase** or **prepositional phrases** in each of the sentences.

Answers are on page 224.

Examples
An adult body consists **of** <u>206 bones</u>.
Newborn babies have **over** <u>300 bones</u>.

1. Some of the bones in a baby grow together during childhood.

2. Muscles pull on your bones and help you move.

3. Bone marrow is in the center of our bones.

4. Red and white blood cells are made in the bone marrow.

5. These blood cells transport oxygen and help fight disease in our bodies.

Think About It!
Set #3 Our Amazing Human Bodies

Choose a **prepositional phrase** from the **prepositional phrases** listed below to correctly complete each sentence. Write the sentence on the line provided.

Answers are on page 225.

of blood   in our blood vessels   Outside the body   in the hot sun

inside our body   Under our skin   of the human body

Examples

The human body contains about six quarts **of blood**.

A large portion **of the human body** is water.

1. _____ we are covered with a layer of skin.

   _____

2. If we stay too long _____, we will get sunburned.

   _____

3. The temperature _____ is usually 98.6 degrees Fahrenheit.

   _____

4. _____ is a layer of muscles.

_____

5. Blood moves _____.

_____

Careful!

Never use just a *prepositional phrase* as a sentence. A *sentence* must have a <u>subject</u> and a <u>predicate</u> and <u>express a complete thought</u>.

CONJUNCTIONS

Now that you have learned about **prepositions**, let's learn about the other part of speech that helps to *connect* words—**conjunctions**.

WHAT IS A CONJUNCTION?

A **conjunction** is a word that *connects* words. The most commonly used **conjunctions** are listed below:

and
or
but
so

Notice how these **conjunctions** *connect* the words in the following sentences.

USING THE CONJUNCTIONS *And* and *Or*

The **conjunction** *and* means *in addition to*.

Careful!

The conjunction *and* is often used with the adjective *both*.

Both my friends **and** I are learning some science facts.
Both my mother **and** father are from Brazil.
Ms. Vu **and** Ms. Alvarez *both* taught us about the human skeleton.

The **conjunction** *or* means *there is a choice between two things*.

Careful!

The conjunction *or* is often (but not always) used with the adjective *either*.

We are going *either* today **or** tomorrow.
We can *either* go to the zoo **or** to the planetarium.

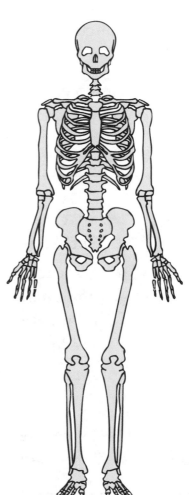

Key Points!

Use the conjunction *and* when you mean *in addition to*. The conjunction *and* is often used with the adjective *both*.

Isis *and* I are walking home from school.
<u>Both</u> she *and* I wait for the school crossing guard to stop traffic.

Use the conjunction *or* when there is a *choice* between two things. The conjunction *or* is often, but not always, used with the adjective *either*.

We can go <u>either</u> to the zoo *or* to the swimming pool.
Do you want to go to the zoo *or* to go swimming?

Let's Try It!
Set #4 Some Properties of Matter

For each sentence below, determine whether the **conjunction *and*** or the **conjunction *or*** should be used to complete the sentence correctly. Write your sentence on the line provided.

Answers are on page 225.

Examples
Iron (and, or) steel are examples of metals.
<u>Iron **and** steel are examples of metals.</u>

Metals can be either shiny (and, or) dull.
<u>Metals can be either shiny **or** dull.</u>

1. Which is the solid form of water, ice (and, or) steam?

   _____

2. Two examples of solids are wood (and, or) metal.

   _____

3. Either wood (and, or) cork will float in water.

   _____

4. Both steel (and, or) iron will sink in water.

   _____

5. "Will a candle sink (and, or) float in water?" asks Ms. Vu.

   _____

USING THE CONJUNCTIONS *BUT* AND *SO*

The **conjunction *but* *connects*** two different ideas or actions that <u>don't go together or agree</u> with each other.

Careful!

When using the conjunction *but*, you usually have to insert a comma (,) after the word written before the conjunction *but*.

I want to learn about the human body, **but** my friends want to learn about the planets.
I studied my spelling words, **but** I still misspelled some words.
I want to play outside, **but** it is raining.

The **conjunction *so*** shows something is the *result* of the first thing happening. It *connects* two *actions*.

Careful!

When using the conjunction *so*, you usually have to insert a comma (,) after the word written before the conjunction *so*.

It was raining, **so** the bus was late.
Juan studied his spelling words, **so** he did very well on the spelling test.
It is late, **so** we have to leave now.

Key Points!

The conjunction *but* <u>connects two different idea or actions</u> that <u>don't go together or agree</u> with each other.

    I want to go swimming, <u>but</u> it is raining.
    I wanted to play baseball, <u>but</u> Hector wanted to play football.

The conjunction *so* shows something is the result of the first thing happening. It <u>connects two actions</u>.

    It is raining, <u>so</u> Papa drove us to school.
    The sun is shining, <u>so</u> we will walk to school.

Let's Try It!
Set #5 Earthquakes

For each sentence below, select the **conjunction** from the **conjunctions** in parentheses ( ) that correctly completes the sentence. Write your sentence on the line provided.

Answers are on page 225.

Examples

We know earthquakes occur, (but, and) what causes them?

We know earthquakes occur, **but** what causes them?

The shaking of the ground is usually not harmful, (so, or) most earthquakes are nothing to worry about.

The shaking of the ground is usually not harmful, **so** most earthquakes are nothing to worry about.

1. Sometimes the ground both rolls (and, so) shakes during an earthquake.

    _____

2. After an earthquake occurs, scientists can tell both how strong it was (but, and) where it started.

    _____

    _____

3. Earthquakes occur in northern California (but, so) not in southern Texas.

    _____

4. I live in Houston, Texas, (so, but) I have never felt an earthquake.

_____

5. I live in northern California, (so, or) I have felt several earthquakes.

_____

Think About It!
Set #6 Hurricanes

Read the following story about hurricanes. <u>Underline</u> each **conjunction**. Refer to the earlier exercises to help you remember which words are **conjunctions**.

Answers are on page 225.

HURRICANES

A *meteorologist* is a person who studies the weather causing hurricanes and other kinds of storms. Hurricanes can be dangerous because they bring both strong winds and rain. I live in the Gulf Coast area, so I have seen hurricanes. Before a

hurricane, people in the hurricane's path must decide either to stay in their houses or to go to another place away from the hurricane's path. I usually stay, but sometimes when there is a dangerous hurricane, I leave town. Before and during a hurricane, you must be careful and stay informed.

Wrapping It Up!

A *preposition* is a word showing how one noun or pronoun is *related* to another noun or pronoun in a sentence. It helps to *connect* the two nouns or pronouns.

The following are some examples of *prepositions*:

of   over   under   to   in   at   on   for

A *prepositional phrase* is a group of words beginning with a *preposition* and ending with a noun or pronoun.

over the bridge   *in* the class   *on* the desk

The *object of the preposition* is the noun or pronoun at the end of the *prepositional phrase*.

over the <u>bridge</u>   *in* the <u>class</u>   *on* the <u>desk</u>

A *conjunction* is a word that *connects* words. The following are the most common *conjunctions*: *and*, *or*, *but*, and *so*.

Obi *and* I are learning about science.
Either Obi *or* I will look through the telescope tomorrow night.
Obi wants to go first, *but* Ms. Vu said I could go first.
It is cloudy tonight, *so* we will not look through the telescope.

Chapter 7

Putting the Finishing Touches on Your Writing

A Chapter about Capitalization and Punctuation

THE UNITED STATES OF AMERICA

TERMS AND DEFINITIONS

Capital Letter: A *letter of the alphabet* that is taller and written differently from its small or lowercase letter.

Person's Title: A word you sometimes put before a person's name or use instead of a person's name.

Punctuation: The use of certain marks to separate words within a sentence and to end sentences.

Punctuation Mark: The *mark* used when you separate words within a sentence or end a sentence.

Comma: A punctuation mark (,) used to separate words.

Dialogue: The words you write to tell exactly what someone said.

Quotation marks: Punctuation marks marking off and showing the exact words of a speaker.

Sentence: A group of words expressing a complete thought. That is, it tells who or what, and it lets you know what happens.

Statement: A sentence telling the reader *about* something.

Question: A sentence *asking* something.

Command: A sentence telling someone *to do* something.

Exclamation: A sentence *showing strong feeling.*

CAPITAL LETTERS AND PUNCTUATION

Congratulations! You have just learned all of the parts of speech, and you know how to write sentences! You are well on your way to becoming a good writer. If you want to become a better writer, there are still a few more things to learn.

Read the following paragraph Obi wrote.

juan and carlos were born in mexico city they are brothers their family moved to the united states seven years ago their parents enjoy it here but they also miss mexico and so at least once a year the family returns to mexico juan and carlos enjoy going to mexico they like to visit with their grandmother rosa and their cousins ramonna jorge max and maria

That paragraph was hard to read, wasn't it? Why? The parts of speech were used correctly, and the words were correctly spelled. What was the problem?

The problem was incorrect **punctuation** and **capitalization**. There were no **capital letters** in the first word of a sentence and in the proper nouns. In addition, there was no **punctuation** for sentence endings and for separating things and actions.

Now, let's read the paragraph after Obi has *correctly* **punctuated** it and *correctly used* **capital letters**.

Juan and Carlos were born in Mexico City. They are brothers. Their family moved to the United States seven years ago. Their parents enjoy it here, but they also miss Mexico, and so at least once a year the family returns to Mexico. Juan and Carlos enjoy going to Mexico. They like to visit with their grandmother Rosa and their cousins Ramona, Jorge, Max, and Maria.

Much better, isn't it?

Learning some rules for **punctuation** and **capitalization** will keep your writing from being confusing like Obi's first paragraph was.

Fortunately, Shakespeare is here to help you learn some useful **punctuation** rules and show you when to use **capital letters**. While Shakespeare is teaching you about **punctuation** and **capitalization**, he will also be telling you about some *interesting places in the United States*.

Let's get started!

WHAT IS A CAPITAL LETTER?

Capital letters have an important job in the English language. The following table lists both the lowercase letters and the **capital letters** of all twenty-six letters of the English alphabet. Notice how the **capital letters** are taller and are written differently than their lowercase letters.

Lowercase Letter	Capital Letter
a	A
b	B
c	C
d	D
e	E
f	F
g	G
h	H
i	I
j	J
k	K
l	L
m	M
n	N
o	O
p	P
q	Q
r	R
s	S
t	T
u	U
v	V
w	W
x	X
y	Y
z	Z

USING CAPITAL LETTERS

Now that you have seen the **capital letters**, let's learn when you need to use them so that your writing will be easy to understand.

SENTENCE BEGINNINGS

Always start with a **capital letter** when you write the **first word in a sentence**. This helps your reader understand you are *beginning a sentence*.

<u>M</u>y family lives in Houston, Texas.
<u>W</u>e have lived there for 2 years.
<u>T</u>he elementary school is two blocks away.
<u>S</u>ometimes it is very hot in Houston.

 **Let's Try It!**

Set #1 Some Cities in the Northeastern United States

Use **capital letters** to write each of the sentences correctly on the line provided. Make sure each of your sentences begins with a **capital letter**.

Answers are on page 226.

Examples

my cousin lives in New York City.
<u>My cousin lives in New York City.</u>

we are going to visit him this winter.
<u>We are going to visit him this winter.</u>

he said it is cold there in the winter.
<u>He said it is cold there in the winter.</u>

i hope it snows!
I hope it snows!

1. two large cities in the northeast are New York City and Boston.

_____

2. another large city in the northeast is Philadelphia.

_____

3. some northeastern states have many large cities.

_____

4. two of the largest cities in Pennsylvania are Pittsburgh and Philadelphia.

_____

5. the largest city in Massachusetts is Boston.

_____

PROPER NOUNS

In Chapter 1, you learned a **noun** is a word naming a *person*, *place*, or *thing*. Most nouns are **common nouns**. A **common noun** names *any* person, place, or thing. **Proper nouns** name a *specific* or *particular* person, place, or thing. The first letter of a **proper noun** must be **capitalized**.

Common Noun	Proper Noun
city	Boston
person	Jorge
school	Martin Luther King Jr. Elementary School
month	January
country	United States
state	Texas
building	Empire State Building
ocean	Pacific Ocean
holiday	Christmas
lake	Lake Michigan

Ugo lives in the city of **Boston**.

He is a student at **Martin Luther King Jr. Elementary School**.

The **United States** has fifty states.

The **United States** stretches from the **Atlantic Ocean** to the **Pacific Ocean**.

Christmas is in **December**.

December is the twelfth month of the year.

We went swimming in **Lake Michigan**.

Careful!

Always capitalize the pronoun *I*, no matter where it appears in your sentence.

I am a student in Ms. Wu's class.
Juan and **I** enjoy her class.
"It was **I** who made the cake," said Claudelle.

Let's Try It!

Set #2 The Midwestern States

Correctly write each of the sentences on the line provided below the sentence. Make sure to **capitalize** the pronoun *I*.

Answers are on page 226.

Examples

My brother obi and i live in ohio.
My brother <u>**O**bi and **I** live in **O**hio.</u>

ohio is east of illinois.
<u>**O**hio is east of **I**llinois.</u>

cleveland and cincinnati are two large cities in ohio.
<u>**C**leveland and **C**incinnati are two large cities in **O**hio.</u>

1. obi and i live in cleveland, ohio.

   _____

2. chicago is in the state of illinois.

   _____

3. chicago is one of the largest cities in the united states.

   _____

4. the city of chicago is along the shoreline of lake michigan.

_____

5. the city of cleveland is along the shoreline of lake erie.

_____

MONTHS, DAYS, AND HOLIDAYS

You must **capitalize** the first letter in the names of the **months**, **days**, and **holidays**. The table below lists the **months** of the year, the **days** of the week, and some of the **holidays** we celebrate during the year that you must **capitalize.**

Months	Days	Holidays
January	Sunday	Christmas
February	Monday	Thanksgiving
March	Tuesday	Fourth of July
April	Wednesday	Labor Day
May	Thursday	Memorial Day
June	Friday	Ramadan
July	Saturday	Hanukah
August		Kwanzaa
September		Cinco de Mayo
October		
November		
December		

The first day of the week is **Sunday**.
The first month of the year is **January**.
Labor Day is in the month of **September**.
October is the tenth month of the year.
Saturday is my favorite day of the week.

Let's Try It!
Set #3 Thanksgiving Vacation in California

Correctly write each of the sentences on the line provided below the sentence. Make sure each of the **months, days,** and **holidays** in the sentence begins with a **capital letter**.

Answers are on page 226.

Examples

we are going to visit my cousin in california next november.
We are going to visit my cousin in California next November.

On monday, my cousin sent us photographs of san francisco.
On Monday, my cousin sent us photographs of San Francisco.

we are going to california over the thanksgiving holiday.
We are going to California over the Thanksgiving holiday.

1. we will arrive in california on wednesday.

_____

2. we will spend thanksgiving in san francisco.

_____

3. thanksgiving is always on a thursday.

_____

4. i would like to spend christmas in california.

_____

5. christmas is always on december 25th.

_____

 **Key Points!**

The *first word of a sentence* must be *capitalized*.

> *The* largest city in Florida is Miami.
> *My* aunt lives in El Paso, Texas.

The pronoun *I* is always capitalized.

> Carlos and *I* are going to Florida.
> My mother and *I* will visit my aunt in Texas.

Proper nouns must be capitalized.

> My cousin *Jorge* goes to *Key Middle School*.
> My friend *Isis* is from *Mexico*.

Remember to capitalize the *months*, *days*, and *holidays*.

> *Christmas* is on *December* 25th.
> *New Year's Day* is on *January* 1st.

Think About It!

Set #4 Christmas Vacation in California

Select words from the list of words below and finish the paragraph about Obi's vacation. Make sure you **capitalize** the first letters of words that

- begin a sentence, or

- are proper nouns, or

- are months, days, or holidays

Answers are on page 226.

cleveland	ohio	december	pacific ocean
ugo		friday	san francisco

Examples

Ugo and Obi live in <u>Cleveland</u>, <u>Ohio</u>.
They are going to California in <u>December</u>.

    Obi and his brother ____ are taking a trip to California with their parents. The brothers left Cleveland on Tuesday. They are driving to _____, California. They plan to arrive in California on _____. They want to see the whales swimming in the _____.

BOOK TITLES

You must **capitalize** the first letter of the **first word**, the **last word**, and **all of the important words in a book title.** Always <u>underline</u> a **book title.**

<u>Once Upon a Banana</u>

<u>Move Over, Rover!</u>

<u>The Little Red Hen</u>

WAR AND PEACE

Careful!

Always capitalize the word *Is* in a book title. It is an important verb.

Let's Try It!

Set #5 Books about the United States

Use **capital letters** to correctly write the **titles of the books** on the line provided.

Answers are on page 227.

Examples

<u>exploring california</u>	<u>Exploring California</u>
<u>texas is big!</u>	<u>Texas Is Big!</u>
<u>tales from the mojave desert</u>	<u>Tales from the Mojave Desert</u>

1. swimming in the pacific ocean

_____

2. my life in the american west

_____

3. hello from florida!

_____

4. from ocean to ocean: the united states

_____

5. the desert is alive!

_____

A Person's Title

What is a **person's title**? A **person's title** is a word you sometimes put _before_ a person's name or use _instead of_ a person's name. You must **capitalize** the first letter in a **person's title.**

Mr. Gomez	**D**r. Montoya
Ms. Wu	**M**om
Uncle Jorge	**D**ad
Aunt Isis	**P**apa

Mr. Gomez is a teacher in our school.

Mom and **Papa** always take us to the library.

Uncle Jorge and **Aunt** Isis live across the street from us.

Ms. Vu and **Dr**. Montoya are teaching us about cities in the United States.

Let's Try It!
Set #6 Visiting Florida

Read the following paragraph about Isis's trip to Florida. Rewrite the story on the lines provided. **Capitalize** the **titles** of the people in the story.

Answers are on page 227.

Examples

aunt Isis is my mother's sister.

<u>A</u>unt Isis is my mother's sister.

She and uncle Jorge travel to many places.

<u>She and </u><u>U</u><u>ncle Jorge travel to many places.</u>

This summer, aunt Isis and uncle Jorge are traveling to Florida. I wish I could go. My teacher, ms. Wu, said it is very pretty in Florida. Juan's teacher, dr. Montoya, said they have lots of oranges and nice beaches in Florida. mommy and papa said maybe we can visit Florida next year.

_____

_____

_____

_____

 Key Points!

Capitalize the <u>first</u>, the <u>last</u>, and <u>all of the important</u> words in a *book title*.

Always *capitalize* the verb *is* when it appears in a *book title*.

<u>A Star Is Born</u>

Always <u>underline</u> *book titles*.

<u>My Life as a Cowboy</u>

Always capitalize a *person's title*.

Mama   *Uncle* Jorge   *Ms.* Wu

Think About It!
Set #7 Ms. Wu's Travels

Correctly write each sentence on the line provided below. **Capitalize** all the words that should begin with **capital letters**.

Answers are on page 227.

Examples

ms. Wu grew up in san francisco, california.
<u>M</u>s. Wu grew up in <u>S</u>an <u>F</u>rancisco, <u>C</u>alifornia.

She and her brother alex could see the pacific ocean.
She and her brother <u>A</u>lex could see the <u>P</u>acific <u>O</u>cean.

"the geography of the united states is a good book to read," said ms. Wu.
"<u>T</u>he <u>G</u>eography of the <u>U</u>nited <u>S</u>tates is a good book to read," said <u>M</u>s. <u>W</u>u.

1. ms. Wu moved from california to houston, texas.

_____

2. she lives next to her aunt lucy on main street.

_____

3. ms. Wu wants to travel to florida to see the atlantic ocean.

_____

4. "i have been to chicago and seen lake michigan," she said.

_____

5. she is planning on spending christmas in new york city.

_____

PUNCTUATION

So far in this chapter, you have learned about **capital letters** and how they make your writing easier to understand. Now it is time to learn about something else to make your writing easier to understand—**punctuation**.

WHAT IS PUNCTUATION?

Punctuation is the use of certain marks called **punctuation marks** to separate words within a sentence and mark the ends of sentences. Using **punctuation marks** separates the *thoughts*, *actions*, *names*, and *ideas* you have written about, so it is easier for your reader to understand what you have written.

PUNCTUATION WITHIN A SENTENCE

USING COMMAS TO SEPARATE WORDS

The *punctuation mark* most frequently used in writing is the **comma**. **Commas** have many different uses. Their main use is to *separate* words such as *nouns*, *adjectives*, and *verbs* in a **series**.

Nouns in a Series

Use a **comma** to separate <u>three or more *nouns* or *pronouns*</u> in a series.

California, *Oregon*, and *Washington* border the Pacific Ocean.

Virginia, *North Carolina*, and *Florida* border the Atlantic Ocean.

Mona, *she*, and *I* are going to travel to Texas.

Adjectives in a Series

Use a **comma** to separate <u>three or more *adjectives*</u> in a series.

"I think Texas is the *most interesting*, *biggest*, and *strangest* state," Mario said.

Obi's brother is *taller*, *older*, and *funnier* than Obi.

A lion is *faster*, *stronger*, and *bigger* than a house cat.

Verbs in a Series

Use a **comma** to separate <u>three or more *verbs*</u> in a series.

I like to *read*, *hear*, and *learn* about the states in the United States.

Maria *walked* home, *ate* a snack, and then *worked* on her homework.

It *rained*, *thundered*, and *turned* dark during the thunderstorm.

Careful!

If possible, try to avoid having <u>too many</u> nouns, adjectives, or verbs in a *series*. Using too many of these words in a series can confuse your reader.

Let's Try It!

Set #8 The Southern States

Add **commas** to correctly punctuate each sentence.

Answers are on page 227.

Examples

Alabama, Mississippi, Florida, and Georgia are southern states.

Mr. Gonzales has *flown* over, *driven* through, and *hiked* through many of the southern states.

Florida is the *most tropical,* *wettest,* and *hottest* of the southern states.

1. In the summer, the weather in the southern states is humid hot and rainy.

2. Miami Orlando and Tallahassee are cities in Florida.

3. I want to visit Disneyworld go to the beach and fly a kite when I am in Florida.

4. Alabama Louisiana and Texas are also southern states.

5. We flew into Texas drove a car to Florida and then rode on a boat in the Atlantic Ocean.

Key Points!

Use a *comma* (,) to separate <u>nouns</u>, <u>verbs</u>, or <u>adjectives</u> in a *series*.

<u>Nouns in a Series</u>
I have lived in *San Salvador, Houston,* and *Dallas.*

<u>Verbs in a Series</u>
Maria *runs, skips,* and *walks* on her way to school.

<u>Adjectives in a Series</u>
Rex is a *big, brown,* and *furry* dog.

USING COMMAS IN DIALOGUE

Dialogue is the words you write to tell *exactly what someone said*. When you write a **dialogue**, use a **comma** to separate <u>what</u> is said from <u>who</u> said it.

"Hawaii is our fiftieth state," Ms. Vu said.

"Alaska is our largest state," I said.

Ugo said, "Pennsylvania and New York belonged to the original thirteen colonies."

Let's Try It!
Set #9 Living in Florida

Use **commas** to punctuate the **dialogue** of Ms. Wu and Hector correctly.

Answers are on page 227.

Examples

"I used to live in Vietnam," said Ms. Wu.

"I was born in Mexico," said Hector.

Ms. Wu replied, "Now we both live in Florida."

1. "I enjoy living in Florida" said Hector.

2. "I enjoy it here also" replied Ms. Wu.

3. Hector said "I like the warm weather, and I like living close to Disneyworld."

4. "I enjoy going to the beaches" said Ms. Wu.

5. Hector said "I don't like the hurricanes that sometimes come through here."

QUOTATION MARKS

Quotation marks separate and show the *exact words of a speaker*. In the previous exercise set about **commas** and **dialogue**, you saw how the writer placed **quotation marks** at the <u>beginning</u> of what the speaker said and at the <u>end</u> of what the speaker said.

Careful!

Remember to add a comma to *separate* <u>what was said</u> from <u>who</u> <u>said it</u>.

"I have always lived in St. Louis," Jorge said.

"I moved here from Vietnam," said Pham.

Jorge said, "We live in the largest city in Missouri."

Let's Try It!
Set #10 Rivers of the United States

Add **quotation marks** and **commas** to punctuate the following sentences correctly.

Answers are on page 228.

Examples
Elsa said I would like to learn about rivers.
Elsa said, "I would like to learn about rivers."

Ms. Wu asked What is the longest river in the United States?
Ms. Wu asked, "What is the longest river in the United States?"

The Missouri River is the longest river answered Hector
"The Missouri River is the longest river," answered Hector.

1. The Missouri River is over 2500 miles long said Ramona

2. Elsa exclaimed That's long!

3. The Mississippi River carries the most water because it is much wider and deeper than the Missouri River said Ms. Wu.

4. She said The United States has over 250,000 rivers.

5. Rivers provide us with water for drinking and farming said Ramona.

SPECIAL USES FOR COMMAS

Between the Day and Year in a Date

Use a **comma** to separate the **day** and the **year** when you write a date.

Matt was born on December 14, 1986.

Katie was born on December 13, 1984.

The Declaration of Independence was signed on July 4, 1776.

Between the City and the State in a Location

Use a **comma** to separate the **city** and the **state** when you write a location.

I live in San Diego, California.

Uncle Jorge is from El Paso, Texas.

We moved here from New York, New York.

Let's Try It!
Set #11 Dates and Places

Use **commas** to write each of the sentences correctly.

Answers are on page 228.

Examples

Obi was born on December 11, 1998.

He was born in Houston, Texas.

Nadia moved here from Chicago, Illinois.

We visited Denver, Colorado, on April 23, 2007.

1. Ramona was born on November 1 1999.

2. She lives in Miami Florida.

3. We moved to Cleveland Ohio on May 10 2007.

4. I have lived in Los Angeles California and Seattle Washington.

5. Have you ever been to Dallas Texas?

 **Key Points!**

Use a *comma* and *quotation marks* when you are writing *dialogue*.

A *comma* and *quotation marks* separate <u>what was said</u> from <u>who said it</u>.

"I would like to visit Los Angeles, California," said Pham.
"My family is taking a trip to Denver, Colorado," said Gabe.

Use a *comma* to separate the *day* from the *year* in a date.

June 11, 2007   April 15, 2005

Use a *comma* to separate the *city* from the *state* when you write a location.

Miami, Florida   Atlanta, Georgia

PUNCTUATION AT THE END OF A SENTENCE

Now that you have learned about **punctuation** within a sentence, it's time to learn about the last bit of **punctuation** in this chapter—**punctuation at the end of a sentence.**

In Chapter 1, you learned that a **sentence** is a group of words containing a *subject* and a *predicate* and expressing a *complete thought*.

In Chapter 1, you also learned about the **four types of sentences**, but let's quickly review them.

A **statement** is a sentence **informing** the reader about something. A **statement** requires a *period* (.) at the end.

The Missouri River is the longest river in the United States.

Houston is a city in Texas.

Georgia is a southern state.

A **question** is a sentence **asking** something. A **question** requires a *question mar*k (?) at the end.

Is Mississippi a southern state?

What state is the city of St. Louis in?

Where is the Empire State Building?

A **command** is a sentence **telling** someone to do something. A **command** requires a *period* (.) at the end of it.

Please close the window.

Study your spelling words.

Juan, hold your sister's hand.

An exclamation is a sentence **showing strong feeling.** An **exclamation** requires an *exclamation point* (!) at the end.

Watch out!

Don't touch that!

Be careful!

 **Key Points!**

A *statement* requires a *period* (.) at the end.
　　Atlanta is the largest city in Georgia.
　　Jackson is the capital city of Mississippi.

A *question* requires a *question mark* (?) at the end.
　　What is the largest city in Ohio?
　　Is Columbus the capital city of Ohio?

A *command* requires a *period* (.) at the end.
　　Please hand in your homework.
　　Close the window, please.

An *exclamation* requires an *exclamation point* (!) at the end.
　　Watch out, Carlos!　　Stop!

Let's Try It!

Set #12 More about the Rivers of the United States

Add the correct **punctuation mark** to the end of each sentence. Write the **type of sentence** on the line provided.

Answers are on page 228.

Examples

The Rio Grande River flows into the Gulf of Mexico.	**Statement**
Where does the Mississippi River flow?	**Question**
Please answer the question.	**Command**
Watch out, Pham!	**Exclamation**

1. The Mississippi River also flows into the Gulf of Mexico

   _____

2. Where does the Ohio River flow

   _____

3. The Ohio River flows into the Mississippi River

   _____

4. Stop, Juan

   _____

5. Please read the paragraph on page 2

   _____

Think About It!

Set #13 Famous Places

On the line provided below the sentence, correctly write each sentence using **capital letters** and **commas**.

Remember: Use correct punctuation to end the sentences.

Answers are on page 228.

Examples

where is the empire state building asked ricardo
"Where is the Empire State Building?" asked Ricardo.

pittsburgh pennsylvania has a professional football team: the pittsburgh steelers

Pittsburgh, Pennsylvania has a professional football team: the Pittsburgh Steelers.

it is in new york city he answered
"It is in New York City," he answered.

the golden gate bridge is in san francisco california
The Golden Gate Bridge is in San Francisco, California.

everglades national park is in homestead florida
Everglades National Park is in Homestead, Florida.

1. we went to disneyworld on august 1 2007

_____

2. baltimore maryland is famous for its seafood

_____

3. st. louis has a professional baseball team: the st louis cardinals

_____

4. did you visit the grand canyon national park in arizona

_____

5. we saw the ohio river when we were in pittsburgh pennsylvania

_____

Wrapping It Up!

Always start with a *capital letter* when you write the <u>first word in a</u> <u>sentence</u>.

<u>T</u>he capital of Texas is Austin, Texas.

The pronoun *I* must always be *capitalized*.

Ugo and *I* walked to school.

The first letter of a <u>proper noun</u> must be *capitalized*.

Rosa   Michigan   Grand Canyon

You must *capitalize* the first letter in the names of <u>months</u>, <u>days</u>, and <u>holidays</u>.

December   Monday   Thanksgiving

Capitalize the first letter of the <u>first word</u>, the <u>last</u> <u>word</u>, and <u>all of the important words</u> in a *book title*.

<u>Once Upon a Banana</u>

Always *capitalize* the verb <u>is</u> in a *book title*.

<u>A Star *Is* Born</u>

Always *capitalize* a person's title.

<u>M</u>ama   <u>M</u>s. Wu   <u>D</u>r. Montoya   <u>U</u>ncle Jorge

Use a *comma* (,) to separate, <u>nouns</u>, <u>verbs</u>, or <u>adjectives</u> in a *series*.

<u>Nouns in a Series</u>
I have visited *New York City*, *Phoenix*, and *San Francisco*.

<u>Verbs in a Series</u>
Maria *runs*, *skips*, and *walks* on her way to school.

<u>Adjectives in a Series</u>
Felix is a *small*, *black*, and *furry* cat.

Use a *comma* when you write a <u>dialogue</u> to separate <u>what is said</u> from <u>who said it</u>.

Remember: Use *quotation marks* to mark off and show the <u>exact words of the speaker</u>.

"Alaska is our forty-ninth state," said Hector.

Use a *comma* to separate the <u>day</u> from the <u>year</u> when you write a <u>date</u>.

October 10, 1954

Use a *comma* to separate the <u>city</u> from the <u>state</u> when you write a <u>location</u>.

Los Angeles, California

Use the correct *sentence endings* in your writing.

A *statement* requires a *period* (.) at the end.

> Baton Rouge is the capital city of Louisiana.

A *question* requires a *question mark* (?) at the end.

> What is the largest city in Texas?

A *command* requires a *period* (.) at the end.

> Be careful when you cross the street.

An *exclamation* requires an *exclamation point* (!) at the end.

> Watch out, Carlos!

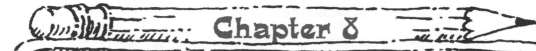

Chapter 8

Do You Want to Know about Paragraphs?

A Chapter about Writing Paragraphs

TERMS AND DEFINITIONS

Paragraph: A group of sentences explaining one topic in detail.

Sentence: A group of words stating a complete thought.

Topic Sentence: A sentence telling the main idea of a paragraph.

Support Sentence: A sentence helping to explain the main topic of a paragraph.

Summarizing Sentence: A sentence expressing how you feel or think about the main topic or repeating the main topic using different words.

Transitions: A word or phrase helping to connect *sentences*.

PARAGRAPHS

In this chapter, Shakespeare will help you learn to write paragraphs, and at the same time, talk to you about *school*.

WHAT IS A PARAGRAPH?

A **paragraph** is a group of sentences explaining one topic in detail. The sentences in the paragraph help you understand what the paragraph is about. Do you remember from Chapter 1 what a **sentence** is?

A **sentence** is a group of words expressing a complete thought. That is, it tells *who* or *what* and the *action performed*. A **sentence** must begin with a capital letter and must end with a period, question mark, or exclamation point.

How many sentences should there be in a **paragraph**? There should be enough sentences to explain the *main idea* of the **paragraph**. That means a paragraph should have at least three sentences. Every paragraph should have a *topic sentence*, one or more *support sentences*, and one *summarizing sentence*.

PARTS OF A PARAGRAPH

The **topic sentence** explains the *main idea of the paragraph*, and it is usually the first sentence.

A **support sentence** *adds more information* about the *main topic*.

The **summarizing sentence** is always the last sentence in a paragraph. You can write the **summarizing sentence** in a way to *repeat* the topic sentence but in different words. You can also write it to express *how you feel* or *what you think* about the main topic.

TOPIC SENTENCE

A good **topic sentence** names the main person, place, or thing described in the paragraph. It should tell your reader the *main idea*.

Read the paragraph below and find the **topic sentence**.

Spring is Juan's favorite time of the year. In the spring, Juan has fun planting flowers with his classmates to attract honeybees. He likes spring better than any other season of the year!

This paragraph has three sentences. The first sentence—*Spring is Juan's favorite time of the year*—is the **topic sentence**. It tells you the paragraph is about *spring* and what is special about *spring*. It is "Juan's favorite time of the year."

The second sentence is a **supporting sentence** because it explains *why* spring is his favorite time of the year:

"In the spring, Juan has fun planting flowers with his classmates to attract honeybees."

The last sentence is the **summarizing sentence** because it *summarizes* or reviews the paragraph.

Now, let's look at another example:

Lisa wants to be a school principal when she grows up. A school principal is in charge of the whole school. I think Lisa will enjoy telling the teachers what to do.

In this paragraph, the **topic sentence** is the first sentence: "*Lisa wants to be a school principal when she grows up.*" This is the *main topic* of the paragraph. It shows the paragraph is about *Lisa* and what is special about her. "*She wants to be a school principal when she grows up.*"

The second sentence is the **supporting sentence** because it tells what a school principal does.

The last sentence is the **summarizing sentence** because it summarizes the paragraph by expressing what the writer *thinks*.

Careful!

To find the *topic sentence*, first, you should ask yourself: <u>What is the paragraph about?</u> Next, find the sentence answering your question. That sentence is the *topic sentence*.

Let's Try It!
Set #1 School Friends

Read the paragraphs below and <u>underline</u> the **topic sentence** in each sentence.

Answers are on page 229.

Examples

<u>*Ramona is Leticia's best friend.*</u> *They met on the first day of school, and they both like to jump rope. I think they will be friends forever!*

<u>*John and Roberto are crazy about basketball.*</u> *They like to play basketball all the time. They are good at it and hope one day to play for the school team.*

1. Manuel and Myra grew up in the same small town in Peru. They are now in my class and are friends. It is amazing how they were both placed in the same class!

2. I know twin sisters who are best friends. They are in the second grade. It is fun to see how much alike they are.

3. My music teacher and my English teacher are very good friends. I see them in the cafeteria laughing and talking. I wonder if all their friends are teachers.

4. Pham and I like to play softball. She is a pitcher, and I play second base. We both play on the same softball team. We play softball every chance we get.

5. I met Stephanie on the first day of school. She just moved to my school. I helped Stephanie find her classroom, and now we play together at recess every day.

SUPPORT SENTENCE

A **support sentence** adds more information about the *main topic*. This information makes the paragraph more interesting. Sometimes, we refer to the **support sentences** as "details" of the *main topic*.

A sentence is a **support sentence** only if it adds information about the *main topic*. Something you write can be true, but if it does not add information about the *main topic*, it is not a **support sentence,** and it should be removed from the paragraph.

Let's Try It!
Set #2 Teachers at My School

Read the sentences below. You will find a **topic sentence** and two other sentences. From the two additional sentences, <u>underline</u> the **support sentence.**

Answers are on page 229.

Examples

Ms. Smith is our favorite art teacher. Her car is blue and white. In her class, we can paint with watercolors.

Topic sentence:

Ms. Smith is our favorite art teacher.

Her car is blue and white.

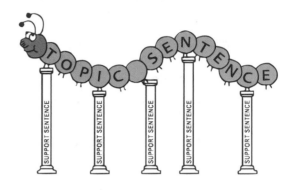

    This sentence is not a **support sentence**. It has nothing to do with the topic sentence, and it should be removed from the paragraph.

In her class, we can paint with watercolors.

    This sentence is a **support sentence** because it further explains why Ms. Smith is our favorite art teacher.

1. The computer teacher has her own laptop. She is from Indiana and likes to wear jeans. She hooks up her laptop to a projector to show us how to use different computer programs.

    Topic sentence:
    The computer teacher owns her own laptop.

    She is from Indiana and likes to wear jeans.
    She hooks up her laptop to a projector to show us how to use different computer programs.

2. Mrs. Lin makes English so much fun! In her class, we learn English by singing songs and playing games. English is Mrs. Lin's second language.

Topic sentence:
Mrs. Lin makes English so much fun!

In her class, we learn English by singing songs and playing games. English is Mrs. Lin's second language.

3. Learning about dinosaurs is Mr. Peyton's hobby. He is our science teacher, and he likes to talk about meat-eating dinosaurs. Mr. Peyton came to our school four years ago.

Topic sentence:
Learning about dinosaurs is Mr. Peyton's hobby.

He is our science teacher, and he likes to talk about meat-eating dinosaurs.
Mr. Peyton came to our school four years ago.

4. We learn history in Mrs. Rider's social studies class. She likes to read magazines. In her class, we learn about Native American tribes.

Topic sentence:
We learn history in Mrs. Rider's social studies class.

She likes to read magazines.
In her class, we learn about Native American tribes.

5. Everyone at school likes Ms. Alana, our third-grade math teacher. She lets us do problems on the chalkboard. Ms. Alana just went to the beach.

Topic sentence:
Everyone at school likes Ms. Alana, our third-grade math teacher.

She lets us do problems on the chalkboard.
Ms. Alana just went to the beach.

Careful!

The above sentences do not form a paragraph because they lack a *summarizing sentence*.

SUMMARIZING SENTENCE

The last sentence in a paragraph is the **summarizing sentence**. You can write the **summarizing sentence** in a way to *repeat* the topic sentence but in different words. You can also write it to express *how you feel* or *what you think* about the main topic.

In the following paragraphs, the underlined sentences show three different ways to write a **summarizing sentence**.

Rebecca goes to school because she wants to be a scientist. She loves learning about rocks in our science class. <u>It is important to go to school to become what you want to be.</u> (Repeats topic sentence)

My dad attends night school. He likes to study math. <u>He loves going to school just like me.</u> (Expresses how you feel)

Mario attends our school because it is close to where he lives. His house is only 15 minutes away. <u>Because he lives near the school, he can get home very quickly.</u> (Expresses what you think)

Let's Try It!
Set #3 School Days

Read the sentences on the next two pages. Choose the **summarizing sentence** at the end of this exercise best fitting the *topic sentence* and *support sentences*. Write the **summarizing sentence** on the line provided.

Answers are on page 229.

167

Examples

Esther, who is my best friend, is in my class. We met in kindergarten, and we have been buddies ever since. Esther helps me with math, and I help her with reading. <u>*Having my best friend in class with me makes the day so much fun!*</u>

Taking the bus to school can be a hassle. This morning, I woke up late, got dressed quickly, and made it to the bus stop as the bus was pulling up. <u>*I was lucky to ride the bus to school today.*</u>

The **summarizing sentences** for the above examples are:

Having my best friend in class with me makes the day so much fun!
I was lucky to ride the bus to school today.

1. Mr. Yi is very strict, and he gives us a lot of homework. He is our fourth-grade teacher. He says homework will help us understand what we learn in class.

   _____

2. Alberta's favorite subject is reading. She loves to read books and learn new words. Sometimes she imagines she is part of the story in the book she is reading.

   _____

3. I like to eat lunch at the cafeteria on Tuesdays and Thursdays. Every Tuesday, we have spaghetti and meatballs. Every Thursday, we have hamburgers and French fries. The lunches served on the other three days are just not as good.

   _____

4. Recess is important to my friends. During recess, we can go to the playground or play soccer or basketball.

Summarizing sentences:

She loves reading more than anything else!
I love Tuesday's lunch and Thursday's lunch.
We look forward to his homework assignment every day.
Doing homework is important to me.
They look forward to recess every day.

 **Key Points!**

A *paragraph* is a group of sentences explaining one topic in detail.

A *paragraph* should have at least three sentences. Every paragraph should have a *topic sentence*, one or more *support sentences*, and one *summarizing sentence*.

The topic sentence explains the main idea of the paragraph, and it is usually the first sentence.

A *support sentence* adds more information about the *main topic*.

The *summarizing sentence* is always the last sentence in a paragraph. You can write the *summarizing sentence* in a way to *repeat* the topic sentence but in different words. You can also write it to express *how you feel* or *what you think* about the main topic.

WRITING PARAGRAPHS

WRITING A TOPIC SENTENCE

You just learned that a **paragraph** has a *topic sentence,* one or more *support sentence(s),* and a *summarizing sentence.* Now, let's learn how to write a **paragraph** starting from the beginning.

To begin, you start with the **topic sentence**. You can write the **topic sentence** using the following procedure:

First, select a topic you want to write about. Let's say you want to write about *our school cafeteria*; however, *"our school cafeteria"* is a broad topic. You need to make it more specific because a **paragraph** should be about only *one topic in detail*.

Second, select what it is about *our school cafeteria* that you want to write. Suppose you want to write about *breakfast* and you want to write about the good breakfast the cafeteria serves.

Let's summarize what we have so far:

Subject: The school cafeteria
What do you want to write about the subject?
How good breakfast is

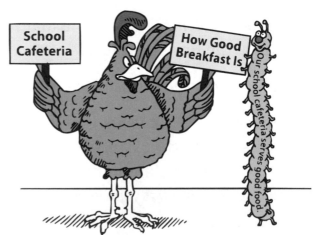

Third, since you know the subject and what you want to write about the subject, you can write the **topic sentence**.

Topic sentence:
Our school cafeteria serves a good breakfast.

Let's look at another example:

Subject: Our Assistant Principal
What do you want to write about the subject?
She is in charge of discipline.

Topic sentence:
Our Assistant Principal is in charge of discipline.

Let's Try It!
Set #4 School Activities

First, read the *subject* and decide *what you want to write about the subject.* Next, on the line provided, finish writing the **topic sentence.**

Answers are on pages 229–230.

Examples

Subject: Our school choir
What do you want to write about the subject?
They sing beautifully

Topic sentence:
Our school choir sings beautifully.

Subject: My science project
What do you want to write about the subject?
How difficult it was

Topic sentence:
My science project was very difficult.

1. Subject: Grades

   What do you want to write about the subject?
   You earn good grades if you study

   Topic sentence:
   Those who study _____.

2. Subject: The library

   What do you want to write about the subject?
   Books for third-graders

   Topic sentence:
   Our library has many good _____.

3. Subject: The gym

   What do you want to write about the subject?
   It has a big basketball court

   Topic sentence:
   _____ has a big basketball court.

4. Subject: The computer lab

What do you want to write about the subject?
We have only seven computers

Topic sentence:
Our computer lab _____.

5. Subject: The cafeteria

What do you want to write about the subject?
Fourth-graders eat at 11:30 a.m.

Topic sentence:
_____ eat in the cafeteria at 11:30 a.m.

WRITING A SUPPORT SENTENCE

Support sentences provide information or details about the topic.
Support sentences answer one or more of the following questions
about the topic: *Who? Where? What? When? Why? How?*

One of the sentences below is a
support sentence; the other is a *topic
sentence.*

My friend found a ladybug!

She was looking at a plant, and
she found a beautiful ladybug.

The first sentence has a subject: *"My friend."* Also, it tells you about *my friend*: *she found a ladybug!* Thus, the first sentence, "My friend found a ladybug!" is the **topic sentence**.

The second sentence is the **support sentence** because it gives us details about how it happened: "My friend was looking at a plant, and she found a ladybug."

Let's Try It!
Set #5 Recess

In this exercise, you will find two sentences. One sentence is the **topic sentence**; the other is the **support sentence**. On the line provided, write a **T** if the sentence is a **topic sentence**. Write an **S** if the sentence is a **support sentence**.

Answers are on page 230.

Examples

Muriel and Robert like to jump rope. __T__
They compete to see who can jump for a longer time. __S__

The gym teacher lent us a soccer ball. __S__
We played soccer at recess today. __T__

1. Six boys and two girls were playing soccer. _____
   The score was tied 1 to 1. _____

2. The teacher let us play tic-tac-toe on the chalkboard. _____
   It rained today, so we had recess inside. _____

3. Ming and Robert made several trips to the water fountain. _____
   They were thirsty because it was hot. _____

4. Susan bounced the ball so hard it landed on the roof! _____
Our basketball game ended suddenly. _____

5. We could not play on the swings today. _____
The swings had puddles of water under them because of the rain.

_____

WRITING A SUMMARIZING SENTENCE

The **summarizing sentence** reminds your reader what your paragraph is about. You can do this by retelling the topic sentence in a different way. Also, you can write the **summarizing sentence** to show your reader *how you feel* or *what you think* about the main topic.

Below are examples of the three ways of writing a **summarizing sentence**.

Topic sentence:
My friend found a ladybug!

Support sentence:
She was looking at a plant, and she found a beautiful ladybug.

Summarizing sentence (*It retells the topic in a different way.*)
My friend is lucky to have found a ladybug.

Summarizing sentence (*It tells your reader how you feel.*)
I wished I could have found a ladybug.

Summarizing sentence (*It tells your reader what you think.*)
I think my friend is a lucky girl!

Let's Try It!
Set #6 More about Recess

In this exercise, write in the space provided the **summarizing sentence** fitting the *topic sentence,* and the *support sentences*. Also, write one of the following letters in the blank space provided:

D if the **summarizing sentence** states the topic in a <u>different</u> way.

F if the **summarizing sentence** tells how the author <u>feels</u>.

T if the **summarizing sentence** tells what the author <u>thinks</u>.

Answers are on page 230.

Examples

Julie and Natasha like jumping rope. Julie jumps faster than Natasha. She began jumping rope when she was three years old. However, <u>I think they are both good at jumping rope.</u>

Julie likes science, but Natasha prefers math. _____
I think they are both good at jumping rope. __T__

We are learning to play basketball at recess. Our teacher, Ms. Sinclair, is teaching us. She played basketball in college. <u>Learning to play basketball is hard, but it is also a lot of fun.</u>

Basketball is played in high school. _____
Learning to play basketball is hard, but it is also a lot of fun. __F__

1. Six boys were playing baseball. They used cones as bases. Johnnie hit the ball, ran very fast, and got to second base.

   _____

   Playing ball is fun! _____
   The field is behind the school. _____

2. It rained today, so we had recess inside. The teacher let us play Scrabble.

   Some of my friends played checkers.

   _____

   My friends take turns playing. _____
   I like recess on rainy days! _____

3. We made many trips to the water fountain. It was very hot during recess. The temperature was above 90 degrees.

   _____

   There was not a cloud in the sky. _____
   You need to drink plenty of water when the weather is hot. _____

4. Our basketball game ended suddenly. Susan bounced the ball so hard it landed on the roof. Ugo looked surprised! We were all disappointed the game ended so fast.

   _____

   I wish we could get our ball back. _____
   We are not allowed to climb on the roof. _____

5. We could not play on the swings today. They had puddles of water on the ground under them because of the rain. The teacher was afraid our shoes would get muddy.

_____

The swings were off limits today! _____
We could throw sand on the puddles and play! _____

CONNECTING SENTENCES IN PARAGRAPHS

TRANSITIONS

Transitions are words or phrases _connecting_ sentences. They make your writing easier to understand because your reader can better understand what you are thinking.

Use the word list below to help you connect your ideas.

To show <u>location</u>: _above, across, around, between, by, inside, next to, outside, over_

To show <u>time</u>: _about, after, at, before, during, finally, later, next, soon, then, today, until, yesterday_

To show <u>order</u>: _first, second, third_

To <u>add information</u>: _again, also, and, besides, finally, further, next_

To <u>compare</u>: _also, as, like_

To <u>contrast</u>: _but, however, yet_

To <u>conclude</u>: _because of, finally, in conclusion, therefore_

To <u>emphasize a point</u>: *again, in fact, to repeat*

To <u>illustrate</u>: *for example, for instance, such as*

The paragraph below has **transitions** helping to connect the sentences.

I do not like vegetables. First, *they taste funny.* Second, *they smell awful.* However, *my mom says they are good for me!* Therefore, *I close my eyes, hold my breath, and eat them anyway!*

The writer used *first* and *second* to show order. Then, she used *however* to change from complaining about vegetables to what Mom had to say. Last, she used *therefore* to write the conclusion: "I close my eyes, hold my breath, and eat them anyway!"

Let's Try It!
Set #7 School Activities

In this exercise, read the paragraph and add the selected **transitions** on the line provided.

Answers are on page 230.

Examples

Transitions: *After, However,* and *Now*

Before class today, Ms. Crystal, our Reading teacher, asked me to join the Book Club. I was so excited I told my friend Carlos. <u>However</u>, he

became sad because he was not invited. <u>After</u> class, I talked to Ms. Crystal about Carlos. She said he could join the Book Club too. <u>Now</u>, we are both very happy!

Transitions: *However* and *Yesterday*

We are having student elections at our school. <u>Yesterday</u>, my classmates elected me class representative to the student council. I was surprised they picked me instead of Johnny who was class representative last year. <u>However</u>, I think I will do a terrific job!

1. Transitions: *In fact*, *Yet*, and *Usually*

Presidents' Day is always celebrated at our school. _____, Mrs. Jones always decorates the bulletin board with a picture of President Washington surrounded by red, white, and blue ribbons. _____, our cafeteria serves cherry pie, but this year, we had cherry ice cream instead! ____, I wish we could have had cherry pie.

2. Transitions: *Again*, *Finally*, and *However*

Our drama teacher, Ms. Wu, told us the good news! Our class has been selected to put on the school play this year. We are performing "Three Little Pigs." Michael, Leticia, and I will play the parts of the three little pigs. _____, when Ms. Wu asked for someone to play the part of the big, bad wolf, no one volunteered. She talked to everyone individually, but nobody wanted the part. _____, she asked the whole third-grade class, but still, no one wanted to be the wolf. _____, a fourth-grader volunteered for the part!

3. Transitions: *Soon* and *Lately*

Our school choir is small, but it sounds terrific! Later this year, we will sing at our school pageant. _____, we have been practicing on Tuesday afternoons. _____, we will start practicing three times a week because we want everything to be perfect for the big show.

4. Transitions: *Now*, *At first*, and *For instance*

My mom met my teacher, Mr. Tam, at the school's Open House. _____, I was nervous about their meeting, but my mom was very happy when she came home. _____, she gave me a big scoop of ice cream that night. _____, I am glad they met!

5. Transitions: *Thus* and *However*

Science Fair week is here. _____, students are busy working on their projects. My project, the life cycle of a butterfly, is good, but Marvin's working ant farm is even better! _____, I still hope my project wins first prize.

Wrapping It Up!

A *sentence* is a group of words stating a complete thought.

A *paragraph* is a group of sentences explaining one topic in detail. It consists of at least three sentences: one *topic sentence,* one or more *support sentence(s),* and one *summarizing sentence.*

A *topic sentence* tells the main idea of the paragraph.

A *support sentence* helps explain the main topic of the paragraph.

A *summarizing sentence* expresses how you feel or what you think about the main topic, or repeats the main topic using different words.

Transitions are words or phrases connecting sentences.

Chapter 9

How Do You Write a Story?
A Chapter about Story Writing

TERMS AND DEFINITIONS

Steps to Writing a Story: Prewriting, Drafting, Revising, Editing, and Publishing

Prewriting: All of the planning you must do to write your story for the first time. This step involves *brainstorming* and *outlining*.

Brainstorming: Writing, in about 10 minutes, everything that comes to your mind about your story.

Outlining: Organizing all the information and ideas you have gathered into an outline.

Drafting: Writing sentences and paragraphs using all the ideas you have gathered in the *story outline*.

Revising: Reading the story again to make sure that what you have written makes sense.

Editing: Checking for spelling and grammatical errors in your story.

Publishing: Writing your story with all the changes from *Revising* and *Editing*.

DECIDING WHAT TO WRITE ABOUT

Choosing a topic to write about is not easy. Luckily, in elementary school, your teacher assigns you a topic. However, if you have to choose a topic, make sure it is a topic you know something about and one that interests you.

THE WRITING PROCESS

Let's say your teacher asks you to write a story about *an adventure you had*. How would you write it? What would you do first? In this chapter, Shakespeare is going to teach you how to write a five-paragraph story, while at the same time, teach you some interesting things about the *San Diego Zoo*.

Together, he and you are going to write a story about *an adventure*. To write a story, you need to follow these steps: *Prewriting, Drafting, Revising, Editing, and Publishing.*

PREWRITING

Prewriting is all the planning you must do to write the *draft* of a story. It includes the following:

- Brainstorming

- Selecting three *topics* from the brainstorming words or phrases to write three paragraphs. Then, grouping the details matching each *topic*.

- Answering the five *W*s (*Who, What, Where, When, Why)* and the *How* of the story.

- Outlining the story

Careful!

Hold off doing the *prewriting* exercises until you have read the whole *prewriting* section. You may have to read this section two or three times before you are ready to do the exercises.

BRAINSTORMING

The purpose of **brainstorming** is to think of enough *topics* about *one central theme* so you are able to select *three topics.* You will write a paragraph about each of the three topics. These three paragraphs, also called *body* paragraphs, are in addition to the *introduction* and *conclusion* paragraphs.

When you **brainstorm**, you write down everything that comes into your mind about the topic of your story. Write down only words or phrases. You do not want to spend your time, now, writing full sentences.

Take no more than 10 minutes to write all the thoughts that come into your mind about the topic of your story.

Let's Try It!
Set #1 Brainstorming

On the left-hand side, you will see a **brainstorming** example about an *adventure* Shakespeare had. Read it carefully. Use Shakespeare's example to **brainstorm** about your topic. Use the lines provided below to write your work.

Words shown in *italics* let you know what Shakespeare is *thinking about* during the **brainstorming** process.

Brainstorming words or phrases—"An adventure I had":

Shakespeare's Brainstorming	**Your Brainstorming**

What does the word <u>adventure</u> mean?

Unexpected
Does not happen all the time _____
Could be fun _____
Different _____
_____

What adventures have I had?

Beach _____
Camping _____
Zoo _____
Water park _____

(Shakespeare) I think I will write about <u>the day I was left behind at the zoo</u>.

_____

(You) I think I will write about _____

On the next page, under the heading "What happened at the zoo?" Shakespeare wrote all the words or phrases describing his adventure at the zoo.

On the right-hand side, write all the words or phrases describing **your** adventure. Where it says *"What happened_____,"* write the name of **your adventure.**

What happened <u>at the zoo</u>?

aunt invited us
cousins came along
drove to San Diego
art exhibit
zoo
family left me behind
talking squirrel
saw polar bears and pandas
Su Lin
walked
waited
saw my brother and sister
glad to see me
exciting adventure
ice cream cones

What happened _____

_____
_____
_____
_____
_____
_____
_____
_____
_____
_____
_____
_____
_____
_____

If you are having difficulties coming up with words or phrases describing things that happened during your real adventure, or an imagined adventure, ask yourself the following questions:

Who was with me during my adventure?

_____

What did I do during my adventure?

_____

When did my adventure happen?

_____

Where did my adventure take place?

_____

Why did my adventure happen?

_____

How did my adventure happen?

_____

Now, you may transfer _words or phrases_ from your answers to these questions into the brainstorming Set #1 space above.

If you are still having problems finding words or phrases to describe your adventure, share the title of your adventure with friends and ask them to help you come up with words to describe it.

SEPARATING INTO _TOPICS AND DETAILS_

In Chapter 8, you learned you needed a _topic sentence_, a _support sentence(s)_, and a _summarizing sentence_ to write a paragraph.

Let's review what a _topic sentence_ and a _support sentence_ are.

A _topic sentence_ tells your reader the main idea of the paragraph.

A _support sentence_ helps to explain or clarify the main topic of a paragraph.

In the next exercise, you will be looking for words or phrases to help you write a _topic sentence_ for a paragraph.

You will also be looking for words to help you write *support sentences*. We refer to these words as the *details* of the topic.

For example:

Read this portion of a brainstorming list for a *picnic*.

hot dogs

food

Fourth of July

chips

buns

soda

When you look at the list, you can read the following:

hot dogs—a *detail* of food (telling us what kind of food)

food—a *possible topic* for a paragraph (broad topic)

Fourth of July—a *detail* of food (when we had the food)

chips—a *detail* of food (what kind)

buns—a *detail* of food (what kind)

soda—a *detail* of food (what kind)

Remember, when you select a *possible topic*, you must be able to write a paragraph about it. If what you select as a *possible topic* is too specific, you might not have enough information to write a paragraph.

From the above **brainstorming**, you could write the following *topic sentence:*

We had a variety of *food* for our Fourth of July picnic.

Then, you could use the words *hot dogs, chips, pickles,* and *soda* to write *support sentences* for the *topic sentence.* For example,

My dad cooked the *hot dogs* on the grill. Then, he put them on toasted *buns,* and squeezed mustard and ketchup on them. Mom put the *chips* in a big bowl so we could grab a handful at a time. The *soda* was put on ice, in a big bucket, for everyone to enjoy.

All of the above sentences support the *topic sentence* "We had a variety of *food* for our Fourth of July picnic."

Let's Try It!
Set #2 Selecting Three Possible Topics for Three Paragraphs

In this exercise, you will see, on the left-hand side, the *words* or *phrases* Shakespeare wrote for the brainstorming exercise in Set #1. Three of the words or phrases have **PT** written in front of them.

Shakespeare selected these phrases as *three* possible topics for his three paragraphs. He thought he could write a paragraph about each one of them.

In the first column provided under "Your brainstorming words," rewrite all the words or phrases you came up with in Set #1 Brainstorming.

In the second column provided, write **PT** if the word or phrase is a *possible topic* for a paragraph. Remember, you need three *topics* for the three body paragraphs you will write in *Drafting*.

Shakespeare's Brainstorming Words   Your Brainstorming Words

aunt invited us __PT__   _____ _____
cousins came along _____   _____ _____
drove to San Diego _____   _____ _____
art exhibit _____   _____ _____
zoo _____   _____ _____
family left me behind __PT__   _____ _____
talking squirrel _____   _____ _____
saw polar bears and pandas __PT__   _____ _____
Su Lin _____   _____ _____
walked _____   _____ _____
waited for them _____   _____ _____
saw my brother and sister _____   _____ _____
glad to see me _____   _____ _____
exciting adventure _____   _____ _____
ice cream cones _____   _____ _____

Now you should have your three *possible topics* for your three paragraphs. If you do not have them, brainstorm more ideas or ask someone to help you.

GROUPING DETAILS BY TOPICS

The next step is to group all the words in the brainstorming exercise around each of the *possible topics*.

Let's Try It!

Set #3 Grouping the Details by Possible Topics

The *possible topics* Shakespeare selected are shown in boxes, with *detail* words shown right below. The *detail words* come from Set #2 above. Remember, these *detail words* go with each of the topics in the boxes.

Read through the whole **prewriting** process before attempting this exercise. Remember: Paragraph #1 is the Introduction Paragraph.

Paragraph #2

Aunt Clara invited us

drove
cousins
art exhibit
zoo

Paragraph #2

_____
_____
_____
_____

Paragraph #3

wanted to see the bears and the pandas

polar bears
pandas
Su Lin

Paragraph #3

_____
_____
_____

Paragraph #4   **Paragraph #4**

family got on
the bus and
left me

walked
talking squirrel   _____
what to do   _____
saw them   _____
glad to see me   _____
exciting   _____
ice cream cones   _____

If you don't have at least three details for each topic, brainstorm some more or ask someone to help you.

THE FIVE Ws AND HOW

Answering *Who, What, Where, When, Why,* and *How* will help you gather information about the theme of your adventure. Also, this information will help you write the introduction paragraph. So let's get started answering these questions.

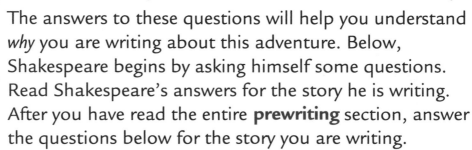

Let's Try It!

Set #4 Answering the Five *Ws* and *How* for Your Story

The answers to these questions will help you understand *why* you are writing about this adventure. Below, Shakespeare begins by asking himself some questions. Read Shakespeare's answers for the story he is writing. After you have read the entire **prewriting** section, answer the questions below for the story you are writing.

Shakespeare's Adventure	Your Adventure

1. Who was involved in my adventure?

Cousins Mario and Beatrix, my older brother Rex, and my sister Elizabeth.

_____
_____
_____

2. What was my adventure?

I was left behind when the family boarded the bus.

_____
_____

3. When did it happen?

During my summer vacation

_____
_____

4. Where did it happen?

At the San Diego Zoo

_____
_____

5. Why did my adventure happen?

I went to pick up my quarter and missed the bus.

_____
_____

6. How did it happen?

We were about to board a double-decker bus, when I dropped a quarter. I went to pick it up, and when I got back, the bus was gone.

_____
_____
_____
_____
_____

195

Story Outline

The purpose of the **story outline** is to organize, in one place, all the information you have gathered. The **story outline** will help you write the *draft* of your story.

Below we will discuss the information needed for the *introduction* paragraph, the three *body* paragraphs, and the *conclusion* paragraph.

Introduction Paragraph

Start the **introduction paragraph** with an interesting *topic sentence*. This sentence can be a question, a feeling, a dialogue, or a statement about what is going on.

The *support sentences* should include information about the *setting* of your story, which is the *time*, the *place* where the story happened, and the *mood*. Also, include the *main characters* of your story in one of your *support sentences*.

Finally, include some information about the *story plot*. The *plot* is what happens during your adventure that makes it interesting to others.

Three Body Paragraphs

For each of the **three paragraphs** in your story, write the *topic sentence* and at least *three details* to use later to write your *support sentences*.

Remember, the *topic sentences* for the three paragraphs are written from the topics in the boxes in Set #3.

Conclusion Paragraph

In the **conclusion paragraph**, include a *topic* sentence tying together the ideas, or *topics*, from the three body paragraphs.

Then, for the *supporting sentences*, retell the topic sentences written below in Set #5, for the three body paragraphs, but use different words.

Finally, finish the **conclusion paragraph** with a sentence summarizing your experience or ending the story for the reader.

Let's Try It!
Set #5 Story Outline

On the left-hand side, Shakespeare has summarized all the information he gathered to write his story. Read it carefully.

On the right-hand side, on the lines provided, write **your** summary of the information you have gathered to write your story.

Introduction—Paragraph #1	Introduction—Paragraph #1
Topic Sentence #1 (To be written later during *drafting*)	**Topic Sentence #1** (To be written later during *drafting*)
Details *Setting* Time: During my summer vacation Place: At the San Diego Zoo Mood: Happy and excited	**Details** Write your story's *setting* Time: _____ Place: _____ Mood: _____

Characters
Cousins: Mario and Beatrix
Elizabeth (my older sister)
Rex (my older brother)
Me

Write your story's *characters*

_____

_____

_____

_____

Plot
I was left behind at the zoo.

Write your story's *plot*

_____

_____

_____

Summarizing Sentence #1
(To be written during *drafting*)

Summarizing Sentence #1
(To be written during *drafting*)

Paragraph #2

Paragraph #2

Topic Sentence #2
My Aunt Clara invited us
to come to San Diego.

Write Topic Sentence #2

_____

_____

_____

Details
drove
cousins
art exhibit

Write Details

_____

_____

_____

198

Summarizing Sentence #2
(To be written during *drafting*)

Paragraph #3

Topic Sentence #3
We wanted to see the polar bears
and the pandas.

Details
zoo
polar bears
Su Lin

Summarizing Sentence #3
(To be written during *drafting*)

Paragraph #4

Topic Sentence #4
My family got on the bus and left me
behind.

Details
walked
talking squirrel
panda
glad to see me

Summarizing Sentence #2
(To be written during *drafting*)

Paragraph #3

Write Topic Sentence #3
_____
_____
_____

Write Details
_____
_____
_____

Summarizing Sentence #3
(To be written during *drafting*)

Paragraph #4

Write Topic Sentence #4
_____
_____

Write Details
_____
_____
_____
_____

Summarizing Sentence #4
(To be written later during *drafting*)

Summarizing Sentence #4
(To be written later during *drafting*)

Conclusion—Paragraph #5
(To be written later during *drafting*)

Conclusion—Paragraph #5
(To be written later during *drafting*)

Writing Topic Sentences #2, #3, and #4 will help you write the supporting sentences for the conclusion paragraph during the drafting step.

Topic Sentence #2
My Aunt Clara
invited us to come to San
Diego.

Write Topic Sentence #2
_____
_____
_____

Topic Sentence #3
We wanted to see the polar bears
and the pandas

Write Topic Sentence #3
_____
_____

Topic Sentence #4
My family got on the bus and left me
behind.

Write Topic Sentence #4
_____
_____

Summarizing Sentence #5
(To be written during *drafting*)

Summarizing Sentence #5
(To be written during *drafting*)

Now, you are ready to go on to the next step—*drafting the story.*

DRAFTING

Drafting is writing sentences and paragraphs from all the *prewriting* ideas you have gathered in your *story outline*.

Let's start with the *introduction paragraph*. This paragraph is a road map to your story. It provides your reader with an idea of what is going to happen in your story.

The *first sentence* of the introduction should catch your reader's attention. Read the possible sentences Shakespeare is considering for his first sentence (also the *topic sentence*) in his introduction:

1. Being left behind by your family at the zoo is no fun at all! (Feeling)

2. "I'm lost, and I don't know what to do!" I said to myself. (Dialogue)

3. Has your family ever left you behind when you went somewhere? (Question)

4. My family left me behind at the zoo. (Declarative)

Shakespeare picked the fourth sentence—a declarative sentence—to start his *introduction paragraph*. Which sentence would you have picked?

Let's Try It!
Set #6 Drafting—Introduction, Paragraph #1

In this exercise, first read the *draft* of *the introduction paragraph* Shakespeare wrote for his adventure. Next, on the lines provided below, write the *draft* for your *introduction paragraph*.

Careful!

You should also write your draft on a sheet of paper. This will make it easier for you to revise and edit your story later.

Remember to use an "attention-getting" first sentence. Also, refer back to Set #5—*Story Outline* to review all the information you have gathered to write this *introduction paragraph*.

There are errors in Shakespeare's **Paragraphs #1**, **#2**, and **#5.** These will be corrected during *revising* and *editing*.

Shakespeare's Introduction—**Paragraph #1**

My family left me behind at the zoo. It happened to me last summer when I went to the San Diego Zoo with my brother Rex, my sister Elizabeth, and my cousins Mario and Beatrix.! It was an experience I will never forget. I was a little scared when my family left me behind but things turned out okay

The **bold** sentence is the *topic sentence* for the paragraph.

Your Introduction—Draft of **Paragraph #1**
(Refer back to Set #5 to review all the information you have gathered.)

_____

_____

_____

Below is Shakespeare's **draft** for his second paragraph. Refer back to Set #5—*Story Outline* to read all the information Shakespeare gathered to write this paragraph.

Let's Try It!
Set #7 Drafting—Paragraph #2

In this exercise, first read Shakespeare's draft of **Paragraph #2.** Next, in the blank spaces provided below, write your draft of **Paragraph #2.**

There are errors in Shakespeare's **Paragraph #2.** He will correct these during *revising* and *editing.*

*It all started one summer afternoon when I heard the phone ring. **It was my Aunt Clara on the phone to invite us to go to San Diego.** She wanted my mother to go with her to an art exhibit at Balboa Park, while my cousins, my older brother Rex, my sister Elizabeth, and I would go to the zoo. My mother said, "Sure, we would be delighted to go!" So, on Monday, we drove from Los Angeles to San Diego.*

The **bold** sentence is the *topic sentence* for the paragraph.

Your draft of **Paragraph #2**
(Refer back to Set #5 to review all the information you have gathered.)

_____

_____

_____

Below is Shakespeare's **draft** for his third paragraph. Refer back to Set #5—*Story Outline* to read all the information Shakespeare has gathered to write his paragraph.

Let's Try It!
Set #8 Drafting—Paragraph #3

In this exercise, first read Shakespeare's draft of **Paragraph #3.** Next, on the lines provided below, write your draft of **Paragraph #3.**

Early Wednesday morning, we were dropped off at the San Diego Zoo. **We wanted to see the polar bears and the pandas.** *Quickly, we headed for the Polar Bear exhibit. A little cub was playing in the cold water while her mother watched her. It was fun to see the bears through the glass wall! Then, my brother said, "I want to see Su Lin!" Who is Su Lin? I asked. "Su Lin is the cute panda bear I told you about," my brother replied. "Okay" said Beatrix, "but we need to take the bus to get there."*

The **bold** sentence is the *topic sentence* for the paragraph.

Your Draft of **Paragraph #3**
(Refer back to Set #5 to review all the information you have gathered.)

_____

_____

_____

Below is Shakespeare's **draft** for his **Paragraph #4**. Refer back to Set #5—*Story Outline* to read all the information Shakespeare gathered to write this paragraph.

Let's Try It!
Set #9 Drafting—Paragraph #4

In this exercise, first read Shakespeare's draft of **Paragraph #4.** Next, on the lines provided below, write your draft of **Paragraph #4.**

When we got to the bus stop, a lot of people were getting in the double-decker bus. I got bored waiting in line, so I started playing with a quarter. Suddenly, I dropped my coin, and it rolled down the pavement. I went to get it, and when I turned around, the bus was gone! There I was, all by myself. **My family got on the bus and left me behind!** *So, I started walking in the same direction as the bus. Suddenly, I heard "pssst," and I turned around. It was a brown squirrel! She said, "You look like you are lost!" I answered, "I am looking for my family. I lost them when they got in the bus." Then, she said, "You need to go back to where you first lost them. They'll come looking for you." I said "thanks" and I ran back to the bus stop and waited. Minutes later, I could see my cousins, and my brother and sister walking toward me. They were so glad to see me! We wandered around for a while looking at the different animals, and then we stopped for chocolate mint ice cream cones.*

The **bold** sentence is the *topic sentence* for the paragraph.

Your Draft of **Paragraph #4**
(Refer back to Set #5 to review all the information you have gathered.)

_____

_____

_____

Now, Shakespeare is going to write the **draft** for the *conclusion* paragraph of his adventure. Refer back to Set #5—*Story Outline* to read all the information you have available to write this paragraph.

Let's Try It!
Set #10 Drafting—Conclusion, Paragraph #5

In this exercise, read Shakespeare's *draft* of his *conclusion*— *Paragraph #5*. Then, on the lines provided below, write your *draft* of your *conclusion—Paragraph #5*.

There are errors in Shakespeare's paragraph. He will correct these during *revising* and *editing*.

Finally, we waited for aunt Clara to pick us up. **It was a very exciting day for me.** *I visited the famous San Diego Zoo I saw polar bears, pandas and other animals. In fact, I met a talking brown squirrel in the few minutes I was seperated from my brother and sister. When mom asked me if I had a good time, I said "You would not believe what happen to me at the zoo today."*

The **bold** sentence is the *topic sentence* for the paragraph.

Your Conclusion, **Paragraph #5**
(Refer back to Set #5 to review all the information you have gathered)

_____

_____

_____

REVISING

Revising is reading the story again to see if it *makes sense*. In this step, you can *add*, *delete*, and *rewrite* words. Also, you can *move* sentences around to correct the order in which events happened.

REPEATED WORDS

Look for **repeated words** in your writing and replace them with *synonyms*. Remember, *synonyms* are words having similar meanings.

Examples

car	automobile	alike	similar
average	common	cheap	no bargain
current	present	daily	day-to-day
dull	boring	fair	adequate
frequent	everyday	good	alright

OVERUSED WORDS

Avoid commonly **overused** words. Use a thesaurus to find synonyms you can use instead.

Examples

Overused word	Consider instead
change	replace
finish	complete
make	construct
nice	pleasant
want	desire

DIALOGUE

Use dialogue to make your story more interesting.

Instead of
My mother said to finish my homework before I watch television.

Consider
"No television until you finish your homework!" said my mother.

SHOW—DON'T TELL

When you write, *you should show—don't tell*. Read the examples below.

Situation	Don't Tell the Reader	Show the Reader
My grandma gave me an apple	I was happy.	I gave her a hug and a great big smile!
My dad told me he was going to take me to a baseball game	I was excited.	I jumped up and down, ran outside, and told my best friend.
I won first prize at the Science Fair	I felt proud.	When I found out, I began to cry.

USE FIVE SENSES

Write sentences in your story that use your five senses to describe what you see, what you smell, what you touch, what you hear, and what you taste. Ask yourself the following questions:

- What did I see?

- What did I smell?

- What did I touch?

- What did I hear?

- What did I taste?

Examples

Below is a description of an apple using your five senses.

Sight	Smell	Touch	Hear	Taste
The apple is bright red and shinny.	It has a sweet, fresh smell.	The skin of the apple is smooth.	When I bit into the apple, I heard a crunching sound.	The apple tasted sweet and tart at the same time.

Now, let's look at how Shakespeare revised his story. Then, you can attempt to revise your story.

Let's Try It!
Set #11—Revising

Below are the first two paragraphs Shakespeare wrote. The sentences are numbered to help you identify them.

Try to find changes to make his **introduction paragraph** better. These changes could include the following:

- Eliminate repeated words.

- Avoid overused words.

- Go from "telling the reader" to "showing the reader."

- Write sentences that use your five senses.

Then, read the **revised** paragraph shown below to see if you can spot the changes.

Shakespeare's Introduction Paragraph

(1) My family left me behind at the zoo. (2) It happened to me last summer when I went to the San Diego Zoo with my brother Rex, my sister Elizabeth, and my cousins Mario and Beatrix. (3) It was an experience I will never forget. (4) I was a little scared when my family left me behind but things turned out okay.

- In sentence #1, *show the reader* what happened in your adventure instead of *telling the reader.* Make the first sentence exciting!

- In sentence #4, *left behind* is mentioned again using the same words as in sentence #1. He should say it in a different way.

Shakespeare's Introduction Paragraph (After Revising)

"I'm lost, and I don't know what to do!" I said to myself. It happened to me last summer when I went to San Diego with my brother Rex, my sister Elizabeth, and my cousins Mario and Beatrix. It was an experience I will never forget. I was a little scared when I got separated from my family, but things turned out okay.

Shakespeare's Second Paragraph

(1) It all started one summer afternoon when I heard the phone ring. (2) It was my Aunt Clara on the phone to invite us to go to San Diego. (3) She wanted my mother to go with her to an art exhibit at Balboa Park, while my cousins, my older brother Rex, my sister Elizabeth, and I would go to the zoo. (4) My mother said, "Sure, we would be delighted to go!" (5) So, on Monday, we drove from Los Angeles to San Diego.

- Use your sense of "feel" in sentence #1 to describe the summer.

- In both the first and second sentences the word *phone* is used. Instead of using the word *phone* twice, use a synonym in one of the sentences or a descriptor telling the reader it is a *phone*.

- We know who Rex and Elizabeth are from the first paragraph, so it should not be repeated in sentence #3.

Shakespeare's Second Paragraph (After Revising)

It all started one hot and humid summer afternoon when I heard ring! ring! It was my Aunt Clara inviting us to come to San Diego. She wanted my mother to go with her to an art exhibit at Balboa Park, while Rex, Elizabeth, and my cousins would go to the zoo with me. My mother said, "Sure, we would be delighted to go!" So, on Monday, we drove from Los Angeles to San Diego.

Notice we did not *indent* the **introduction** paragraph. Why? Because this will be part of the *editing* step to be covered next.

Now it is your turn to **revise** your paragraph based on what you have learned. Read each sentence of your story to make sure it makes sense. If it does not make sense, change it. Use a paper copy of your story to make the changes.

EDITING

Editing is the part of the writing process where you look for spelling and grammatical errors in your story. In this section, you will get a chance to use everything you have learned in this book.

Editing is more effective if you read your story beginning with the last sentence and

Spelling, capitalization, grammar.

work backward because this helps you to focus on each sentence. Check each sentence for the following:

- Spelling errors (use a dictionary)

- Proper capitalization and punctuation (Chapter 7)

- Grammar (Chapters 1–6)

- Sentence structure (Chapter 1)

- Subject and verb in agreement and consistent verb tense (Chapter 4)

Let's Try It!
Set #12—Editing

Below is the last paragraph Shakespeare wrote. Read the paragraph backward, starting with the last sentence.

Try to **edit** the mistakes to make this **conclusion** paragraph better.

Then, read the **revised** paragraph shown below to see if you can identify the changes.

Shakespeare's Conclusion Paragraph

(5) Finally, we waited for aunt Clara to pick us up. (4) It was a very exciting day for me. (3) I visited the famous San Diego Zoo I saw polar bears, pandas and other animals. (2) In fact, I met a talking brown squirrel in the few minutes I was seperated from my brother and sister. (1) When mom asked me if I had a good time, I said, "You would not believe what happen to me at the zoo today."

- **Sentence 1:** Change "mom" to "Mom" (capitalization)

- **Sentence 1:** Change "happen" to "happened" (verb tense)

- **Sentence 2:** Change "seperated" to "separated" (spelling)

- **Sentence 3:** Place a period after Zoo (run-on sentence)

- **Sentence 3:** Add a comma after pandas (punctuation)

- **Sentence 5:** Indent sentence

Shakespeare's Conclusion Paragraph (After Editing)

Finally, we waited for Aunt Clara to pick us up. It was a very exciting day for me. I visited the famous San Diego Zoo. I saw polar bears, pandas, and other animals. In fact, I met a talking brown squirrel in the few minutes I was separated from my brother and sister. When Mom asked me if I had a good time, I said, "You won't believe what happened to me at the zoo today."

Now it is your turn to **revise** your paragraph based on what you have learned in this chapter. Read your story starting with the last sentence of the conclusion paragraph and work your way back to the beginning.

Check each sentence for all the things you have learned. Use a paper copy of your story to make your changes.

PUBLISHING

Publishing is the last step of the writing process. It is also the easiest. You take your story, with all the corrections from *revising* and *editing*, and write it again, this time on a clean sheet of paper. Now, you have a fantastic five-paragraph story!

Wrapping It Up!

The *steps in writing a story* include the following: prewriting, drafting, revising, editing, and publishing.

Prewriting is the planning that prepares you to write the draft of a story. It involves *brainstorming* and *outlining*.

Brainstorming is writing down, in about 10 minutes, everything that comes into your mind about your story.

Outlining requires you to organize all the information you have gathered into a story outline.

Drafting is writing sentences and paragraphs from all of the ideas you have gathered in the *story outline*.

Revising is reading the story again to make sure that what you have written makes sense.

Editing is checking for spelling and grammatical errors in your story.

Publishing is the final step in the writing process. You rewrite your story with all the changes from *revising* and *editing*.

Answer Key

Chapter I What Is There to Know about Sentences?

Set #1 A Trip to the Zoo
1. This is a sentence.
2. This is a sentence.
3. This is not a sentence.
4. This is not a sentence.
5. This is a sentence.

Set #2 More Fun at the Zoo
1. The zoo has a lot of big animals.
2. The tiger cubs follow their mother.
3. The lions and tigers eat only meat.
4. Some of the monkeys are swinging from branch to branch.
5. My friends and I waved to the monkeys.

Set #3 Polar Bears
1. *Where* do polar bears live?
2. *What* color is a polar bear's fur?
3. *How* big are polar bears?
4. *How* many cubs does a polar bear have?
5. *What* should humans not do?

Set #4 Taking Care of a Pet
1. Bonita, walk your dog.
2. My cat is chasing a mouse!
3. Please pour water in your dog's bowl.
4. My dog is huge!
5. Please clean your hamster's cage.

Set #5 Sharks
1. question
2. statement
3. exclamation
4. statement
5. command

Set #6 Butterflies
1. Butterflies
2. The *thorax*
3. Maria and I
4. All butterflies
5. The wings and legs

Set #7 Spiders

1. learned that there are thousands of different kinds of spiders in the world.
2. have eight legs.
3. have six legs.
4. are not insects but rather are arachnids.
5. trap insects in their webs.

Set #8 More about Spiders

1. *Spiders* have eight legs.
2. *Webs* help spiders trap insects.
3. *Arachnid* is another name for spider.
4. *A tiny foot* is at the end of each of a spider's legs.
5. *Thick brushes of hair* cover each of a spider's legs.

Set #9 Eagles

1. Lots of salmon live in the rivers of Alaska. Bald eagles like to eat salmon.
2. The bald eagle is not really bald. It has white feathers on the top of its head.
3. At one time in the English language, the word "bald" meant white, *and* that is why they were named *bald eagles*.
4. A female bald eagle grows to a height of 36 inches. She is taller than the male eagle.
5. Eagles have wingspans of nearly 90 inches. That's long!

CHAPTER 2 HOW DO YOU NAME PERSONS, PLACES, AND THINGS?

Set #1 Rosa and Her Family

1. sister   El Salvador
2. name   Sylvia
3. family   Los Angeles   California
4. Third Street   Los Angeles
5. sister   Rodriguez Elementary School

Set #2 My Family

1. My mother was born in **Panama**.
2. My mother's name is **Maria**.
3. My family lives in **Berkeley, California**.
4. We live on **Haste Street**.
5. I go to **LeConte Elementary School**.

217

Set #3 Living in the United States

1. love   family
2. grandmother   sadness
3. Honesty   family
4. brothers   fun   pool
5. mother   joy   hope

Set #4 More about Families

1. brothers
2. cousins
3. brothers
4. aunts
5. uncles

Set #5 My Family

1. one brother
2. two sisters
3. four aunts
4. four uncles
5. ten cousins

Set #6 Writing Singular and Plural Nouns

1. box   boxes
2. sandwich   sandwiches
3. class   classes
4. wrench   wrenches
5. fox   foxes
6. bush   bushes
7. church   churches
8. mess   messes
9. bench   benches
10. dish   dishes

Set #7 Writing Special Plural Nouns

1. Our teacher read us three stories.
2. My shoes are on my feet.
3. My sister went to two birthday parties.
4. The pie has a lot of cherries.
5. The men were kicking the ball.

Set #8 Using Plural Nouns to Review Sentences

1. brothers   question
2. ladies   exclamatory
3. berries   command
4. churches   statement
5. boxes   question

Set #9 Angelina and Her Family

1. name   Erika
2. family   Texas
3. father   Kenya
4. mother   United States
5. month   October   Halloween

Set #10 Our Relatives

1. mother's
2. father's
3. father's
4. uncle's
5. aunt's

Set #11 Plural Possessive Nouns

1. My uncles' brother is my father.
2. My brothers' names are Obi and Ugo.
3. My sisters' names are Kayla and Karla.
4. The boys' uniforms are red and white.
5. The teachers' desks are messy.

Set #12 My Relatives

1. mother's   S
2. grandmother's   S
3. father's   S
4. father's   S
5. uncles'   P

CHAPTER 3 WHAT CAN YOU USE INSTEAD OF A NOUN?

Set #1 Water Safety

1. me
2. He   me   I
3. You   you
4. It   you   you
5. We

Set #2 Water Safety and Your Family

1. I ride in my uncle's boat.
2. He wears a life jacket.
3. My sister and I wear one too.
4. It can save your life.
5. We should learn about water safety.

Set #3 More Water Safety

1. "She must wear a life jacket," he said.
2. She put on her life jacket.
3. "It will help me float if I fall out of the boat," she said.
4. They should always be with an adult when they are near the water.
5. We enjoy riding in Uncle Jorge's boat.

Set #4 Fire Safety in Our Homes

1. <u>us</u>
2. <u>you</u>
3. <u>her</u>
4. <u>her</u>
5. <u>us</u>

Set #5 Keeping Safe from Fire

1. subject pronoun
2. object pronoun
3. object pronoun
4. subject pronoun
5. object pronoun

Set #6 Crossing a Street

1. <u>My</u> family lives on a street where a lot of cars drive.
2. <u>Our</u> parents walk to school with us every day.
3. Sometimes Papa drives us in <u>his</u> car.
4. He says <u>our</u> safety is very important to Mama and him.
5. <u>Your</u> school crossing guard can help you cross the street safely.

Set #7 Our School Crossing Guard

1. He keeps <u>my</u> friends safe.
2. <u>Our</u> safety is important to him.
3. <u>Our</u> street has many cars on it.
4. The drivers stop <u>their</u> cars.
5. <u>Your</u> crossing guard can help you.

Set #8 Getting Help Crossing the Street

1. <u>We</u>   <u>our</u>
2. <u>My</u>   <u>me</u>
3. <u>He</u>   <u>our</u>
4. <u>He</u>   <u>me</u>   <u>we</u>
5. <u>I</u>   <u>I</u>   <u>me</u>

Chapter 4 Putting Nouns and Pronouns into Action

Set #1 A Trip to the Dentist

1. <u>takes</u>
2. <u>asks</u>
3. <u>said</u>
4. <u>makes</u>
5. <u>told</u>

Set #2 More about Dental Health

1. I don't **eat** a lot of candy because candy can cause cavities.
2. I also don't **drink** a lot of soft drinks because soft drinks can cause cavities.
3. My little sister **watches** me brush my teeth.
4. I **enjoy** showing my little sister how to brush her teeth.
5. My mother **says** both of us will have clean, healthy teeth.

Set #3 Eating and Health

1. is
2. am
3. is
4. was
5. will be

Set #4 Healthy Foods

1. Oranges and grapefruits are fruits.
2. Each piece of fruit I ate was delicious.
3. Oranges and grapefruits are good sources of Vitamin C.

4. Beans are a good source of protein.
5. I am a healthy eater.

Set #5 Eating a Healthy Diet

1. serves   **Action Verb**
2. are   **Linking Verb**
3. provides   **Action Verb**
4. are   **Linking Verb**
5. is   **Linking Verb**

Set #6 Playing Outside Is Good Exercise

1. Maria kicks the soccer ball into the goal.
2. Her friend cheers when the ball flies into the goal.
3. I like to play soccer.
4. My mother says playing soccer is good exercise.
5. I think exercise is fun.

Set #7 Fun Things That Help Us Exercise

1. played
2. skipped
3. jumped
4. waded
5. smiled

Set #8 Keeping Myself Healthy

1. I <u>will exercise</u> every day.
2. I <u>will play</u> outside with my friends.
3. My mother <u>will cook</u> good food.
4. I <u>shall eat</u> fruits and vegetables.
5. I <u>will avoid</u> junk food.

Set #9 Exercise for Good Health

1. <u>walk</u>   **Present Tense**
2. <u>says</u>   **Present Tense**
3. <u>will walk</u>   **Future Tense**
4. <u>played</u>   **Past Tense**
5. <u>makes</u>   **Present Tense**

Set #10 Visiting the Doctor

1. My doctor <u>examined</u> my hearing and breathing.
2. I <u>hear</u> and breathe well.
3. Next year at school, I <u>will read</u> an eye chart to check my eyesight.
4. A doctor's examination <u>helps</u> prevent health problems.
5. I <u>will visit</u> my doctor next September.

CHAPTER 5 HOW DO YOU DESCRIBE AND COMPARE?

Set #1 Our Solar System

1. <u>one</u>
2. <u>many</u>
3. <u>1</u>
4. <u>365</u>
5. <u>88</u>

Set #2 Our Solar System: The Biggest and the Fastest

1. <u>fastest</u>
2. <u>closest</u>
3. <u>closer</u>
4. <u>shorter</u>
5. <u>longest</u>

Set #3 Earth's Neighbors

1. Venus is <u>hotter</u> than Earth.
2. Jupiter is <u>larger</u> than Earth.
3. Jupiter is the <u>largest</u> of the planets in our solar system.
4. Mars has a <u>longer</u> year than Earth.
5. Earth is <u>closer</u> to the sun than Mars.

Set #4 Astronomy: The Study of the Stars and Planets

1. <u>best</u>
2. <u>better</u>
3. <u>good</u>
4. <u>best</u>
5. <u>better</u>

Set #5 Bad Weather on Earth and Elsewhere

1. We had some <u>bad</u> weather yesterday.
2. The weather was <u>worse</u> on Monday than yesterday.
3. The <u>worst</u> weather of all is yet to come!
4. Planets also have <u>bad</u> weather.
5. Of the planets Earth, Mercury, and Mars, Mars has the <u>worst</u> weather.

Set #6 Using *Many* and *Little*

1. I spent a **little** time playing outside.
2. Joanna spent the **least** time playing outside.
3. Hector spent the **most** time playing outside.
4. I ate **less** than Roberto.
5. Roberto ate **more** than I ate.

Set #7 Looking at the Stars

1. Sometimes when it is a <u>**little**</u> cloudy, it is hard to see the stars.
2. I am **careful** when I look through someone else's telescope.
3. You can see **more** stars when you are out in the country than when you are in the city.
4. You see more stars because there is **less** reflected light in the country than in the city. Reflected light makes it hard to see the stars.
5. I think a sky full of stars is the **most beautiful** sight of all!

Set #8 Our Sun

1. <u>**A**</u> star is a ball of burning gas.
2. <u>**The**</u> gas is burning and is very hot.
3. Earth gets its light from the heat of <u>**the**</u> sun.
4. <u>**An**</u> orbit around <u>**the**</u> sun is takes 1 year.
5. All <u>**the**</u> planets in our solar system orbit our sun.

Set #9 *Describing* and *Comparing* the Planets

1. Jupiter has <u>many</u> <u>more</u> moons than Earth.
2. It takes Jupiter and Saturn a <u>very</u> <u>long</u> time to orbit the sun.
3. Venus is an <u>extremely</u> <u>hot</u> planet.
4. Neptune is a <u>very</u> <u>cold</u> planet.
5. Venus is <u>much</u> <u>closer</u> to the sun than Neptune.

Set #10 More about the Planets

1. Earth has <u>very</u> much water in its oceans.
2. Jupiter is a <u>very</u> big planet.
3. Uranus is <u>extremely</u> far from the sun.
4. Mercury is <u>very</u> close to the sun.
5. Mercury is <u>much</u> closer to the sun than Earth is.

Set #11 Looking at the Sun and Planets

1. Jupiter is a very **large** planet.
2. The sun shines **brightly** in our sky.
3. The sun shines **dimly** in Neptune's sky because Neptune is far from the sun.

4. A telescope allows you to look **closely** at the planets.

CHAPTER 6 WHICH WORDS ACT LIKE GLUE?

Set #1 Weather and Climate

1. <u>over</u>
2. <u>between</u>
3. <u>for</u>
4. <u>in</u>
5. <u>of</u>

Set #2 The Human Skeleton

1. Some **of the bones** in a baby fuse together **during childhood**.
2. Muscles pull **on your bones** and help you move.
3. *Bone marrow* is **in the center of our bones**.
4. Red and white blood cells are made **in the bone marrow**.
5. These blood cells transport oxygen and help fight disease **in our bodies**.

Set #3 Our Amazing Human Body

1. <u>Outside the body</u> we are covered with a layer of skin.
2. If we stay too long **in the hot sun**, we will get sunburn.
3. The temperature **inside our body** is usually 98.6 degrees Fahrenheit.
4. <u>Under our skin</u> is a layer of muscles.
5. Blood moves in **our blood vessels**.

Set #4 Some Properties of Matter

1. Which is the solid form of water, ice **or** steam?
2. Two examples of solids are wood **and** metal.
3. Either wood **or** cork will float in water.
4. Both steel **and** iron will sink in water.
5. "Will a candle sink **or** float in water?" asks Ms. Vu.

Set #5 Earthquakes

1. Sometimes the ground rolls **and** shakes during an earthquake.
2. After an earthquake occurs, scientists can tell how strong it was **and** where it started.
3. Earthquakes occur in northern California **but** not in southern Texas.
4. I live in Houston, Texas, **so** I have never felt an earthquake.
5. I live in northern California, **so** I have felt several earthquakes.

Set #6 Hurricanes

Hurricanes

A *meteorologist* is person who studies the weather causing hurricanes **and** other kinds of storms. Hurricanes can be dangerous because they bring both strong winds **and** rain. I live in the Gulf Coast area, **so** I have seen hurricanes. Before a hurricane, people in the hurricane's path must decide either to stay in their houses **or** to go to another place away from the hurricane's path. I usually stay, **but** sometimes when there is a dangerous hurricane, I leave town. Before **and** during a

225

hurricane, you must be careful **and** stay informed.

CHAPTER 7 PUTTING THE FINISHING TOUCHES ON YOUR WRITING

Set #1 Some Cities in the Northeastern United States

1. Two large cities in the northeast are New York City and Boston.
2. Another large city in the northeast is Philadelphia.
3. Some northeastern states have many large cities.
4. Two of the large cities in Pennsylvania are Pittsburgh and Philadelphia.
5. The largest city in Massachusetts is Boston.

Set #2 The Midwestern States

1. Obi and I live in Cleveland, Ohio.
2. Chicago is in the state of Illinois.
3. Chicago is one of the largest cities in the United States.
4. The city of Chicago is along the shoreline of Lake Michigan.
5. The city of Cleveland is along the shoreline of Lake Erie.

Set #3 Thanksgiving Vacation in California

1. We will arrive in California on Wednesday.
2. We will spend Thanksgiving in San Francisco.
3. Thanksgiving is always on a Thursday.
4. I would like to spend Christmas in California.
5. Christmas is always on December 25th.

Set #4 Christmas Vacation in California

Obi and his brother **Ugo** are taking a trip to California with their parents. The brothers left Cleveland on Tuesday. They are driving to **San Francisco**, California. They plan to arrive in California on **Friday**. They want to see the whales swimming in the **Pacific Ocean**.

Set #5 Books about the United States

1. Swimming in the Pacific Ocean
2. My Life in the American West
3. Hello from Florida!
4. From Ocean to Ocean: The United States
5. The Desert Is Alive!

Set #6 Visiting Florida

This summer, **Aunt** Isis and **Uncle** Jorge are traveling to Florida. I wish I could go. My teacher, **Ms.** Wu, said it is very pretty in Florida. Juan's teacher, **Dr.** Montoya, said they have lots of oranges and nice beaches in Florida. **Mommy** and **Papa** said maybe we can visit Florida next year.

Set #7 Ms. Wu's Travels

1. Ms. Wu moved from California to Houston, Texas.
2. She lives next to her Aunt Lucy on Main Street.
3. Ms. Wu wants to travel to Florida to see the Atlantic Ocean.

4. "I have been to Chicago and seen Lake Michigan," she said.
5. She is planning on spending Christmas in New York City.

Set #8 The Southern States

1. In the summer, the weather in the southern states is humid, hot, and rainy.
2. Miami, Orlando, and Tallahassee are cities in Florida.
3. I want to visit Disneyworld, go to the beach, and fly a kite when I am in Florida.
4. Alabama, Louisiana, and Texas are also southern states.
5. We flew into Texas, drove a car to Florida, and then rode on a boat in the Atlantic Ocean.

Set #9 Living in Florida

1. "I enjoy living in Florida," said Hector.
2. "I enjoy it here also," replied Ms. Wu.
3. Hector said, "I like the warm weather, and I like living close to Disneyworld."
4. "I enjoy going to the beaches," said Ms. Wu.

5. Hector said, "I don't like the hurricanes that sometimes come through here."

Set #10 Rivers of the United States

1. "The Missouri River is over 2500 miles long," said Ramona.
2. Elsa exclaimed, "That's long!"
3. "The Mississippi River carries the most water because it is much wider and deeper than the Missouri River," said Ms. Vu.
4. She said, "The United States has over 250,000 rivers."
5. "Rivers provide us with water for drinking and farming," said Ramona.

Set #11 Dates and Places

1. Ramona was born on November 1, 1999.
2. She lives in Miami, Florida.
3. We moved to Cleveland, Ohio, on May 10, 2007.
4. I have lived in Los Angeles, California, and Seattle, Washington.

5. Have you ever been to Dallas, Texas?

Set #12 More about the Rivers of the United States

1. The Mississippi River also flows into the Gulf of Mexico.
   Statement
2. Where does the Ohio River flow?
   Question
3. The Ohio River flows into the Mississippi River.
   Statement
4. Stop, Juan!
   Exclamation
5. Please read the paragraph on page 2.
   Command

Set #13 Famous Places

1. We went to Disneyworld on August 1, 2007.
2. Baltimore, Maryland, is famous for its seafood.
3. St. Louis has a professional baseball team: the St. Louis Cardinals.

4. **D**id you visit the **G**rand **C**anyon **N**ational **P**ark in **A**rizona?

5. **W**e saw the **O**hio **R**iver when we were in **P**ittsburgh, **P**ennsylvania.

CHAPTER 8 DO YOU WANT TO KNOW ABOUT PARAGRAPHS?

Set #1 School Friends

1. <u>Manuel and Myra grew up in the same small town in Peru.</u>

2. <u>I know twin sisters who are best friends.</u>

3. <u>My music teacher and my English teacher are very good friends.</u>

4. <u>Pham and I like to play softball.</u>

5. <u>I met Stephanie on the first day of school.</u>

Set #2 Teachers at My School

1. <u>She hooks up her laptop to a projector to show us how to use different computer programs.</u>

2. <u>In her class, we learn English by singing songs and playing games.</u>

3. <u>He is our science teacher, and he likes to talk about meat-eating dinosaurs.</u>

4. <u>In her class, we learn about Native American tribes.</u>

5. <u>She lets us do problems on the chalkboard.</u>

Set #3 School Days

1. We look forward to his homework assignment every day.

2. She loves reading more than anything else!

3. I love Tuesday's lunch and Thursday's lunch.

4. They look forward to recess every day.

Set #4 School Activities

1. earn good grades.

2. books for third-graders.

3. Our gym
4. has only seven computers.
5. Fourth-graders

Set #5 Recess
1. T, S
2. S, T
3. T, S
4. S, T
5. T, S

Set #6 More about Recess
1. Playing ball is fun! ___F___
2. I like recess on rainy days!
   ___F___

3. You need to drink plenty of water when the weather is hot. ___T___
4. I wish we could get our ball back. ___F___
5. The swings were off limits today! ___R___

Set #7 School Activities
1. In fact, Usually, Yet
2. However, Again, Finally
3. Lately, Soon
4. At first, For instance, Now
5. Thus, However

INDEX